Options Trading for Beginners 2025

Key Strategies for Financial Growth and Minimize Risk

Beau Kincaid

Copyright © 2024 Beau Kincaid.

All rights reserved. No part of this book may be reproduced, stored in a retrieval system, or transmitted in any form by any means—electronic, mechanical, photocopying, recording, or otherwise—without prior written permission from the author, except for brief quotations in reviews or articles.

Table of Content

Table of Content...2
Introduction..8
Understanding Options Basics.............................8
   What Are Options?..9
   Key Terminology in Options Trading....................10
   How Options Work: The Mechanisms Behind Calls and Puts...11
   How Options Differ from Stocks.........................13
   Potential Risks and Rewards..............................14
Chapter 1...17
Why Trade Options?..17
   Understanding Options Basics...........................17
   Risks Associated with Options Trading...............20
   Differences Between Options Trading and Traditional Stock Investing...21
Chapter 2...24
Essential Terminology in Options Trading...............24
   Key Terms in Options Trading............................24
      1. Calls and Puts......................................24
      2. Strike Price..26
      3. Premium...27
      4. Expiration Date....................................28
      5. Volatility..29
      6. Time Decay (Theta).............................30
      7. Intrinsic and Extrinsic Value..................31

Chapter 3 33
Types of Options Contracts 33
Understanding Call and Put Options 33
Differentiating Between American and European Options 36
Impact of Option Type on Trading Strategies 39
Legal Considerations and Risk Management 40

Chapter 4 42
The Fundamentals of Options Pricing 42
Key Elements of Options Pricing 43
  1. Intrinsic Value: The Built-In Worth of an Option 43
  2. Extrinsic Value: The Time and Volatility Premium 45
  3. Time Decay: How Options Lose Value Over Time 47
  4. Implied Volatility: Expectations for Future Price Movement 48

Chapter 5 51
Key Options Trading Strategies for Beginners ... 51
The Purpose of Options Trading Strategies 52
Buying Calls: Profiting from an Anticipated Rise in Stock Price 53
Buying Puts: Gaining from a Predicted Decline in Stock Price 55
Covered Calls: Generating Income on Owned Stocks 56
Protective Puts: Hedging Against Potential Losses 57
When to Use Each Strategy 58

Chapter 6 60

Risk Management in Options Trading.................... 60
    Understanding Risk in Options Trading................. 61
    Stop-Loss Orders: Limiting Potential Losses.......... 63
    Position Sizing: Managing Exposure...................... 64
    Hedging Techniques: Reducing Market Exposure.. 66
    Advanced Hedging Techniques............................ 68
    Regulatory Considerations in Risk Management....70
    Psychological Aspects of Risk Management.......... 72
    Practical Tips for Effective Risk Management........ 73

Chapter 7.. 75
Reading Options Chains and Market Indicators....... 75
    Introduction to Options Chains............................. 75
    Components of an Options Chain......................... 76
    Interpreting Bid-Ask Spreads............................... 79
    Key Market Indicators for Options Trading............ 81
    Practical Example of Reading an Options Chain....83
    Legal and Risk Considerations............................. 83

Chapter 8.. 85
Options Expiration and Assignment......................... 85
    Introduction to Options Expiration and Assignment 85
    Options Expiration: Key Concepts......................... 86
    Assignment Process: How It Works...................... 89
    Potential Impacts on Your Options Positions.......... 91

Chapter 9.. 93
The Role of Volatility in Options Trading................. 93
    Understanding Volatility in Options Trading............ 94
    The Impact of Volatility on Option Pricing............... 96
    Volatility-Based Strategies: Straddles, Strangles, and More.. 97

Using Market Indicators to Predict Volatility.......... 100

Chapter 10... 102

Fundamental Analysis for Options Trading........... 102

Key Components of Fundamental Analysis.......... 103

Fundamental Analysis Strategies for Options Traders... 108

Integrating Market Sentiment into Options Trading.... 111

Sector and Industry Analysis for Informed Options Trading.. 113

Combining Fundamental and Technical Analysis for Options Trading..115

Risk Management and Fundamental Analysis in Options Trading...117

Evaluating Long-Term Market and Industry Trends.... 119

Chapter 11.. 121

Technical Analysis and Charting Basics................. 121

Introduction to Technical Analysis........................ 121

Understanding Stock Charts................................. 122

Popular Chart Patterns... 124

Key Technical Indicators for Options Traders....... 125

Using Technical Analysis for Options Trading...... 128

Combining Technical Indicators with Options Strategies..128

Practical Applications of Technical Analysis in Options Trading... 130

Risk Management in Technical Analysis-Based Options Trading... 132

Limitations of Technical Analysis in Options Trading..

5

Chapter 12 .... **136**
Options Trading Psychology **136**
   Understanding Trading Psychology 136
   Developing Emotional Awareness 138
   The Importance of Discipline in Trading 139
   Cultivating a Winning Mindset 141
   The Role of Risk Management in Trading Psychology 143
   The Importance of Community and Support 144

Chapter 13 .... **147**
Building a Personalized Options Trading Plan **147**
   Understanding the Importance of a Trading Plan. 148
   Setting Goals for Your Trading Plan 149
   Developing Your Trading Strategy 151
   Risk Management in Options Trading 153
   Creating a Review and Adjustment Process 156

Chapter 14 .... **158**
Review of Key Strategies **158**
   Summary of Main Strategies for Beginners 159
   How to Continue Growing as an Options Trader .. 164
   Additional Resources for Continuous Learning 167

Chapter 15 .... **169**
Final Thoughts on Options Trading for Financial Growth **169**
   Staying Informed in a Changing Market 170
   The Role of Practice and Discipline 173
   Setting Yourself Up for Success in 2025 and Beyond 176

Introduction

Understanding Options Basics

In today's rapidly evolving financial landscape, understanding various investment tools is essential for those looking to diversify their portfolio or achieve specific financial goals. Options trading, a strategy once primarily used by professional traders and financial institutions, has become increasingly accessible to individuals thanks to technological advancements and more education on its potential benefits and risks.

This section will provide a foundational introduction to options trading for beginners, covering the essentials: what options are, how they function, common terminology, and the fundamental mechanics of how options work in the market. Equipped with this knowledge, you'll have a solid foundation to explore more advanced strategies, understand the risks involved, and determine if options are suitable for your financial objectives.

What Are Options?

Definition and Basic Concept of Options

An option is a type of financial derivative that gives an investor the right, but not the obligation, to buy or sell an underlying asset, such as stocks, at a predetermined price within a specified timeframe. Unlike owning stock outright, holding an option means you do not own the actual asset until you exercise the option.

Options can be used in various ways: to hedge against losses, to leverage positions for greater profit potential, or to generate additional income on existing investments. The flexibility they offer makes them a valuable tool, but it also requires an understanding of how they operate and the potential risks associated.

The Role of Options in the Financial Market

In the broader financial market, options play a critical role in providing liquidity and flexibility. They allow traders to speculate on price movements without needing to own the underlying asset, making them a popular tool in both bull and bear markets. Options can help manage risk by allowing for strategic positioning, particularly in volatile markets. This appeal has led to their widespread adoption by both individual investors and institutions alike.

Key Terminology in Options Trading

Understanding key terms is essential in navigating options trading. Here are some of the most fundamental concepts:

- **Underlying Asset**: The asset on which an option is based, commonly a stock, ETF, or index. For instance, a call option on Apple Inc. stock gives the buyer the right to purchase shares of Apple.
- **Strike Price**: The predetermined price at which the option holder can buy or sell the underlying asset. If you hold a call option, the strike price is where you'd buy; for a put option, it's where you'd sell.
- **Expiration Date**: Options come with an expiration date, which marks the last day the option can be exercised. After this date, the option expires worthless.
- **Call Option**: This option gives the buyer the right to purchase the underlying asset at the strike price before expiration. Investors typically buy call options if they expect the asset's price to increase.
- **Put Option**: This option gives the buyer the right to sell the underlying asset at the strike price

before expiration. Investors may buy put options if they believe the asset's price will decrease.
- **Premium**: The price paid to acquire an option. The premium represents the cost of having the choice to exercise the option if desired. Premium prices fluctuate based on factors like the underlying asset's price, time to expiration, and market volatility.

How Options Work: The Mechanisms Behind Calls and Puts

Buying Call Options

A call option grants the buyer the right to purchase the underlying asset at the strike price, regardless of its current market price. Here's how it works:

1. **Positioning for a Price Increase**: If you expect the price of an asset (e.g., stock) to rise, purchasing a call option allows you to benefit from this increase. For example, if the stock is trading at $50 and you buy a call option with a strike price of $55, you can buy the stock at $55 even if it rises to $70.

2. **Potential for Limited Losses**: The maximum amount you can lose is the premium paid for the option. If the stock price doesn't reach or exceed the strike price by expiration, you're not obligated to buy the stock, and you only forfeit the premium.
3. **Leveraging Gains**: One of the appeals of call options is leverage. For a fraction of the stock's price (the premium), you can control a larger position and potentially profit more if the price moves favorably.

Buying Put Options

Put options provide the right to sell the underlying asset at the strike price, which is beneficial if you expect the asset's price to decline.

1. **Positioning for a Price Decline**: Suppose a stock currently trades at $60, and you anticipate a drop. Buying a put option with a strike price of $55 allows you to sell it at $55 even if the stock drops to $40. This enables you to hedge against falling prices.
2. **Risk Management**: Put options can act as a form of insurance. If you hold shares of a stock and worry about potential losses, a put option can help offset any decline, as the option increases in value as the stock's price falls.

3. **Profit Potential**: Like call options, put options have a high potential reward-to-risk ratio. If the stock price falls well below the strike price, the option could yield significant profits, especially in highly volatile markets.

How Options Differ from Stocks

Unlike stocks, which represent ownership in a company, options are derivatives—they derive their value from an underlying asset without conferring ownership rights. Here's how options differ from direct stock purchases:

- **Ownership**: When you buy a stock, you own a piece of the company, which can grant voting rights or dividends. Options, however, do not confer any ownership in the underlying asset.
- **Expiration**: Stocks can be held indefinitely, but options have a set expiration date. This time limit adds an element of time-sensitive decision-making in options trading.
- **Risk Profile**: Options can amplify both profits and losses due to their leverage. With stock, you might lose if the price drops, but with options, you could lose your entire premium if the option expires worthless.

- **Flexibility and Strategy**: Options offer more strategic flexibility compared to stocks, with a wide range of strategies (e.g., hedging, income generation, speculation) that appeal to both novice and experienced traders.

Potential Risks and Rewards

Risks of Options Trading

Options trading carries unique risks, primarily due to the expiration dates and potential for total loss of premium. Some key risks include:

1. **Time Decay**: Options lose value as they approach expiration. This time decay affects out-of-the-money options most since they're further from the profit point.
2. **Complexity and Volatility**: Options are more complex than regular stock investments, and their value is highly sensitive to market volatility. This can result in sudden price fluctuations, making them more unpredictable than stocks.
3. **Leverage Risk**: While leverage can amplify profits, it can equally magnify losses. Traders risk losing the entire premium if the market

moves unfavorably, making options riskier for inexperienced investors.

Rewards of Options Trading

When well-understood, options trading offers substantial rewards:

1. **Profit Potential**: With minimal upfront costs, options allow traders to gain more significant exposure to price movements, potentially yielding larger returns than directly purchasing stock.
2. **Flexibility in Strategies**: Options can be tailored for different market views, whether bullish, bearish, or neutral. They can serve diverse purposes, from hedging risk to generating income, which appeals to both conservative and aggressive traders.
3. **Risk Management Tool**: Options provide hedging opportunities, allowing investors to limit losses on other assets in their portfolio. They offer downside protection for those who own the underlying stock, adding an extra layer of security.

Options trading is an exciting and complex tool for diversifying and enhancing financial portfolios, yet it requires a clear understanding of its fundamentals to navigate successfully. While the potential rewards are attractive, the associated risks necessitate a thorough grasp of how options work, why they behave differently from other financial instruments, and the importance of responsible, informed decision-making.

This introduction has laid the groundwork for exploring options trading. In the following chapters, we'll build on these basics, exploring specific strategies, risk management techniques, and advanced approaches to help you succeed in options trading with confidence and control.

Chapter 1

Why Trade Options?

In today's financial landscape, options trading has emerged as a flexible and potentially lucrative investment strategy. While traditional stock investing remains popular, options trading offers unique benefits and risks that appeal to both seasoned investors and beginners seeking more control and strategic opportunities in their portfolios. This chapter explores what makes options trading distinct, detailing its advantages, risks, and its place within a diversified investment strategy. It also includes an introduction to understanding Autism Spectrum Disorder (ASD), with a focus on early recognition and support for parents and educators, shedding light on why boys are more commonly diagnosed and emphasizing the importance of early understanding and action.

Understanding Options Basics

What Are Options?

Options are a type of financial derivative, meaning they derive their value from an underlying asset, usually a stock. Essentially, options give an investor the right, but not the obligation, to buy or sell an asset at a specific price within a predetermined timeframe. The two primary types of options are **call options** (giving the right to buy) and **put options** (giving the right to sell). Each of these has specific roles in investment strategies and different risk and reward potentials.

The key characteristics of options include:

- **Strike Price**: The price at which the option holder can buy or sell the underlying asset.
- **Expiration Date**: The date when the option expires, which is when the holder must decide whether to exercise the option.
- **Premium**: The cost of purchasing an option, which reflects the potential risk and reward of the option.

These elements make options trading different from buying and selling stocks outright. Rather than holding shares and being affected by price movement alone, options provide the opportunity to leverage capital by controlling more shares at a fraction of the price. This leverage can result in amplified gains but also comes with increased risk, as the value of options contracts can fluctuate significantly within short timeframes.

Advantages of Options Trading

Options trading has several advantages that attract both novice and experienced investors. Here are some of the key benefits:

1. Flexibility and Strategy Variety

- Options allow for a variety of strategies, from conservative income generation to high-risk speculation. Investors can use strategies like **covered calls** for income or **protective puts** as a form of insurance against potential losses in their stock holdings. Options also enable **straddles** and **strangles**, which profit from large price swings in either direction, offering strategic flexibility.

2. Leverage and Cost Efficiency

- One of the major attractions of options is their potential for high leverage. With options, an investor can control a larger amount of stock with a smaller capital outlay. For example, rather than buying 100 shares of a stock, an investor could purchase a call option on those shares, giving them exposure to the stock's movement at a fraction of the cost. However, this leverage also increases the potential for losses, making it essential for investors to thoroughly understand the risks involved.

3. Risk Management and Hedging

- Options can be used as a hedge to protect existing investments. For instance, if an investor holds a stock and fears it might decline in value, they can buy a put option to protect against that downside risk. This **protective put** acts as an insurance policy, allowing the investor to mitigate potential losses. Similarly, companies and institutions use options to hedge currency or commodity price fluctuations, showcasing options as a valuable tool for risk management across various markets.

Risks Associated with Options Trading

Options trading comes with its own set of risks that can make it a challenging approach for inexperienced investors:

1. Complexity and Learning Curve

- Unlike traditional stock investing, options involve various moving parts and a steeper learning curve. Investors must understand not only the basics of options contracts but also various trading strategies, volatility, and the concept of **time decay** (how the value of options diminishes as they approach expiration).

2. Potential for Significant Losses

- The leverage that makes options attractive also amplifies potential losses. For instance, if an investor buys a call option and the underlying stock's price falls, the entire premium paid for the option could be lost, leading to a 100% loss of capital. In some cases, options strategies, such as uncovered or "naked" calls, can result in theoretically unlimited losses, underscoring the importance of understanding the risks and avoiding high-risk strategies without adequate experience.

3. Time Decay and Expiration

- Options are time-sensitive assets, and their value decreases as the expiration date approaches—a concept known as **time decay**. This characteristic means that holding an option until it expires can result in the option losing all its value, especially if the underlying asset fails to move favorably.

Differences Between Options Trading and Traditional Stock Investing

Immediate Ownership vs. Derivative Rights

In traditional stock investing, buying a share means you own a piece of the company and can benefit from dividends and stock appreciation. With options, however, investors do not own the underlying asset; they only have the right to buy or sell it at a predetermined price.

Leverage and Potential for Higher Returns

Options trading can offer higher returns relative to stock trading due to leverage. However, this leverage also introduces greater risk, as the entire premium can be lost if the trade goes unfavorably. Traditional stock investing, while often slower in potential returns, may carry less risk in comparison.

Options trading provides unique opportunities for flexibility, leverage, and risk management but comes with substantial risks that must be understood by any investor considering this approach. Informed investors can use options to their advantage, but it's crucial to have a solid foundation in options basics and strategy.

Additionally, a foundational understanding of Autism Spectrum Disorder and gender-based differences in diagnosis equips parents and educators with the tools to support children effectively. Early awareness and intervention are critical to empowering children with ASD, especially boys who may face higher diagnostic rates.

Chapter 2

Essential Terminology in Options Trading

Options trading is a complex and multifaceted form of investing, relying heavily on specialized terminology and concepts. For beginners, understanding the essential terms is critical before engaging with any options strategies or trades. In this chapter, we will explore foundational terms that will serve as the building blocks for a deeper comprehension of options trading. These include terms like calls, puts, strike price, premiums, expiration dates, volatility, and more. By breaking down each term, this chapter will set you up to approach options trading with greater clarity, allowing you to make informed decisions as you progress through this book.

Key Terms in Options Trading

1. Calls and Puts

Call Options and **Put Options** are the two foundational types of options in the market, and understanding these terms is the first step to grasping options trading as a whole.

Call Options

A **call option** grants the holder the right, but not the obligation, to **buy** an asset at a specific price within a predetermined timeframe. This means that if you hold a call option, you expect the price of the underlying asset to **increase** before the option expires, allowing you to purchase it at a lower, predetermined price.

- **Example**: Suppose you purchase a call option for Company XYZ with a strike price of $50. If the price of XYZ rises to $60, you can exercise your option to buy at the lower price of $50, potentially profiting from the difference.
- **Risks**: The price may not rise, or it could even fall, leaving the option worthless. In such cases, you would lose the premium paid to purchase the call option.

Put Options

A **put option**, on the other hand, gives the holder the right to **sell** an asset at a specific price within a predetermined timeframe. Investors buy put options when they expect the price of the underlying asset to **decrease** before the expiration date.

- **Example**: If you buy a put option for Company ABC with a strike price of $40, and the price of

ABC drops to $30, you can sell at the higher strike price of $40, profiting from the difference.
- **Risks**: If the asset's price does not drop as expected, the put option may expire worthless, resulting in a loss of the premium paid.

Together, call and put options enable a range of trading strategies based on anticipated market movements. They are essential tools for speculation and hedging, which we will discuss further in later chapters.

---

2. Strike Price

The **strike price**, sometimes called the **exercise price**, is the price at which an option holder can buy or sell the underlying asset. It is a predetermined figure set when the option is purchased, and it dictates the price point for exercising the option.

- **For Call Options**: The strike price is the price at which the holder can buy the underlying asset.
- **For Put Options**: The strike price is the price at which the holder can sell the underlying asset.

Example of Strike Price in Practice

Suppose you hold a call option on Stock ABC with a strike price of $100, and the stock price rises to $120.

You could exercise the option, buying the stock at the lower strike price and potentially selling at the market price, profiting from the $20 difference.

Importance of Strike Price

Selecting the appropriate strike price is a strategic decision in options trading, as it affects the risk, cost, and potential profit of the trade. Generally, the closer the strike price is to the current market price of the underlying asset, the more likely the option will be exercised.

---

3. Premium

The **premium** is the price you pay to purchase an option. It represents the maximum loss an option buyer can incur, and it compensates the option seller for the risk they assume. Premiums are determined by several factors, including the strike price, the current price of the underlying asset, time to expiration, and market volatility.

Factors Influencing Premiums

- **Intrinsic Value**: The inherent value of the option if exercised at the current market price.

- **Time Value**: The potential for the option to become profitable before expiration.
- **Volatility**: Higher market volatility generally leads to higher premiums.

Example of Premium Calculation

Suppose you buy a call option with a $5 premium on Stock XYZ, with a strike price of $50. You pay $5 per share (typically options contracts cover 100 shares, so the total cost is $500). If the option is not exercised before expiration, your maximum loss is limited to this premium amount.

Premiums play a significant role in determining the potential profitability and risk of each options trade. As a result, they are carefully evaluated in options strategies and risk assessments.

---

4. Expiration Date

The **expiration date** of an option is the final date on which the option can be exercised. After this date, the option becomes void, and the buyer loses any potential right to exercise it. Options can have different durations, from days (weekly options) to years (long-term equity anticipation securities, or LEAPS).

Types of Options Based on Expiration

- **American Options**: These can be exercised at any time up to the expiration date.
- **European Options**: These can only be exercised on the expiration date itself.

Importance of Expiration in Strategy

The expiration date is crucial for determining an option's time value and overall strategy. Options closer to expiration may have a lower time value, making them cheaper to purchase but also riskier, as they have less time to become profitable. Conversely, long-term options provide more time for favorable movements but are usually more expensive due to the increased time value.

---

5. Volatility

Volatility measures the degree to which the price of an asset fluctuates over time. It is a critical factor in determining the premium of an option, as higher volatility implies a greater chance of significant price movement, which could benefit the option holder.

Types of Volatility

- **Historical Volatility**: Reflects the actual past price movements of the asset.
- **Implied Volatility**: Indicates the market's expectation of future price movements, as reflected in the option's premium.

Role of Volatility in Options Trading

Implied volatility is especially significant, as it directly influences the option's premium. Options on more volatile stocks tend to have higher premiums due to the potential for dramatic price changes. High volatility can offer opportunities for profit but also introduces a higher degree of risk, making it essential for traders to understand how it may impact their investments.

---

6. Time Decay (Theta)

Time decay refers to the erosion of an option's value as it approaches its expiration date. This concept, also known as **theta**, impacts the time value of the option, with options losing value as expiration nears.

Example of Time Decay

If you purchase a call option that's set to expire in two months, it will have a higher time value than the same call option with just two days until expiration. This means that options closer to expiration are more likely to lose value quickly, especially if the underlying asset's price remains stagnant.

Managing Time Decay

Time decay is a crucial consideration for options buyers, as they need to be aware of the diminishing time value and the necessity of favorable price movements to compensate for it. For options sellers, time decay can be advantageous, as the decreasing value of the option can increase profitability if the option expires worthless.

---

7. Intrinsic and Extrinsic Value

Intrinsic value and **extrinsic value** make up the total premium of an option.

- **Intrinsic Value**: Represents the actual value if the option were exercised now (i.e., the difference between the current price and strike price).

- **Extrinsic Value**: Represents the additional value of the option due to time remaining until expiration and potential for future profitability.

These components are essential in assessing the option's fair value, and they fluctuate with time, volatility, and the underlying asset's price. Options with only extrinsic value are said to be "out of the money" and may expire worthless if favorable price movement does not occur.

Understanding options terminology is foundational for any aspiring options trader. Terms such as calls, puts, strike price, premiums, expiration dates, and volatility are essential components of every trade and decision made in the options market. Mastery of these terms empowers traders to approach options trading with confidence, making strategic decisions based on a clear understanding of each component.

Chapter 3

Types of Options Contracts

Options trading offers a versatile tool for investors, providing the opportunity to participate in the market with more flexibility than traditional stock investments. While stocks require the outright purchase or sale of shares, options give traders the right, but not the obligation, to buy or sell an asset at a predetermined price within a specific time frame. Understanding the various types of options contracts is essential for any investor looking to leverage the full potential of this financial instrument.

In this chapter, we'll explore the key types of options contracts, including **call** and **put** options, along with **American** and **European** style options. Each of these types carries its own set of benefits, strategies, and potential risks, and knowing how each works can help traders optimize timing and tactics within the options market.

Understanding Call and Put Options

In options trading, the most fundamental differentiation between contract types is **call options** and **put options**.

These contracts form the basis of any options strategy, and knowing how each works is crucial.

Call Options: The Right to Buy

A **call option** provides the buyer the right, but not the obligation, to purchase the underlying asset at a specified **strike price** before the expiration date of the contract. This type of option is generally used by traders who anticipate an increase in the asset's price. Here's a closer look at the key characteristics and components of call options:

1. **Strike Price**: The predetermined price at which the asset can be purchased if the buyer chooses to exercise the option. For call options, the strike price is ideally set below the anticipated future price of the asset.
2. **Premium**: This is the cost of purchasing the option, paid upfront by the buyer. The premium is influenced by factors such as the asset's volatility, time to expiration, and the difference between the strike price and the asset's current price.
3. **Expiration Date**: The date on which the option contract expires. If the option is not exercised by this date, it becomes worthless, and the buyer loses the premium.

4. **Potential Profit and Loss**: The profit potential for a call option is theoretically unlimited, as the price of the underlying asset can continue to rise indefinitely. However, the loss is limited to the premium paid.

Example: Suppose an investor buys a call option on stock XYZ with a strike price of $100, a premium of $5, and an expiration date three months in the future. If XYZ's stock price rises to $120 before expiration, the investor can exercise the option, buying the stock at $100 and selling it at the market price of $120, earning a profit (minus the premium).

Put Options: The Right to Sell

A **put option** gives the holder the right, but not the obligation, to sell the underlying asset at the strike price within the contract's time frame. Put options are typically used when a trader expects the asset's price to decline.

1. **Strike Price**: For put options, the strike price is ideally set above the anticipated future price of the asset, allowing the investor to sell the asset at a higher-than-market value if the option is exercised.
2. **Premium**: Similar to call options, put options require an upfront payment known as the

premium, determined by the same factors: volatility, time to expiration, and the difference between the strike price and the current price.
3. **Expiration Date**: If the put option is not exercised by this date, it expires worthless, resulting in a loss of the premium paid.
4. **Potential Profit and Loss**: The maximum profit for a put option is capped, as the lowest possible value for an underlying asset is zero. Losses are limited to the premium paid if the asset's price remains above the strike price.

Example: An investor purchases a put option on stock ABC with a strike price of $50, a premium of $3, and an expiration date two months in the future. If ABC's stock price falls to $40, the investor can sell the stock at $50, gaining a profit (minus the premium).

Differentiating Between American and European Options

In addition to call and put options, options contracts are categorized into **American** and **European** styles. The difference between these two lies primarily in the timing of when the option can be exercised.

American Options: Flexibility in Execution

American options are the more flexible of the two types, as they allow the holder to exercise the option at any time before the expiration date. This feature is especially beneficial in volatile markets, where timing can greatly impact profit or loss.

- **Benefits**: The ability to exercise at any time provides investors the flexibility to capitalize on favorable price movements immediately, rather than waiting until expiration.
- **Premiums**: Generally, American options may carry slightly higher premiums than European options due to the increased flexibility.
- **Strategy Implications**: American options are commonly used in markets with high volatility or where unexpected news could significantly impact asset prices. The flexibility also makes them a good choice for shorter-term trades.

Example: Suppose an investor holds an American-style call option on a tech stock. If the stock experiences a sudden price spike due to favorable earnings, the investor can immediately exercise the option, capturing the profit without waiting for expiration.

European Options: Defined Exercise Date

European options, by contrast, can only be exercised on the expiration date. This limitation means that even if the underlying asset's price shifts favorably before expiration, the option holder must wait until the designated date to exercise the option.

- **Benefits**: European options often come with lower premiums due to the restricted exercise window, making them a potentially cost-effective choice for investors.
- **Premiums**: Typically lower than American options, reflecting the decreased flexibility.
- **Strategy Implications**: European options are generally more suitable for longer-term strategies where the investor has a specific price target or is confident that the market will move favorably by the expiration date.

Example: An investor purchases a European-style put option on a stock index, expecting it to decrease over the next six months. Even if the index value drops after three months, the investor must wait until the six-month expiration date to exercise the option, which could affect the overall profit.

Impact of Option Type on Trading Strategies

Understanding the nature of call and put options, along with American and European styles, is crucial for developing effective trading strategies. Here's how each type might influence strategy:

1. **Risk Management**: Put options provide a hedge against price declines, useful for investors holding large positions in the underlying asset. Calls, conversely, allow for profit in bullish markets without needing to purchase the asset directly.
2. **Timing and Market Conditions**: American options are suited for markets with high volatility or when immediate action may be required. European options, with their lower premiums, are often used in longer-term strategies where short-term price movements are less critical.
3. **Flexibility**: For active traders, American options offer greater flexibility to respond to market changes, while European options appeal to those with a set price target or a specific expiration date.
4. **Costs and Premiums**: The premium paid for each option impacts profitability. American options may have higher premiums due to

flexibility, making European options more attractive for cost-conscious investors.

Legal Considerations and Risk Management

When engaging in options trading, investors must be aware of the legal and regulatory considerations surrounding options, which are complex financial products often subject to specific regulations.

- **Disclosure Requirements**: Options trading requires an understanding of disclosure documents provided by exchanges, such as the Options Disclosure Document (ODD) in the U.S., which details the risks and requirements.
- **Risk of Loss**: Both call and put options involve the risk of losing the premium paid, with additional potential losses if an option strategy involves more complex setups like spreads.
- **Compliance with Broker Requirements**: Many brokers require investors to meet certain qualifications to trade options, often requiring approval and verification of trading experience and financial knowledge.

By understanding these components—call and put options, American and European styles, and the implications for trading strategies—investors can make more informed decisions and better assess the suitability of options in their overall portfolio. Whether aiming for flexibility with American options or cost-effectiveness with European options, each type presents unique opportunities and risks that should align with one's financial goals and risk tolerance.

Chapter 4

The Fundamentals of Options Pricing

Understanding how options are priced is foundational for any beginner stepping into the world of options trading. Options pricing is a complex blend of market forces, mathematical models, and inherent characteristics of the contracts themselves. For those new to options, these pricing mechanisms can seem daunting, but grasping the basics is essential to making informed, strategic decisions.

This chapter breaks down the key factors that influence the value of an options contract, including **intrinsic and extrinsic value**, **time decay**, and **implied volatility**. By understanding these elements, traders can begin to decode options prices, assess the worth of specific contracts, and recognize how these factors interplay with one another. Knowledge of options pricing allows traders to evaluate if a contract is worth the premium and better predict how that premium may change over time, aiding in more strategic decision-making.

Key Elements of Options Pricing

Options pricing is influenced by several essential elements, each of which contributes to the overall premium or cost of the option. The most fundamental components include **intrinsic value** and **extrinsic value**. These two factors together determine the fair value of an option at any given time.

1. Intrinsic Value: The Built-In Worth of an Option

The **intrinsic value** of an option represents the immediate, inherent worth of the option based on its strike price and the current market price of the underlying asset. An option has intrinsic value if exercising it at that moment would result in a profit.

Calculating Intrinsic Value for Calls and Puts

The intrinsic value is calculated differently for call options (right to buy) and put options (right to sell).

- **Call Option Intrinsic Value**: For a call option, intrinsic value exists when the current stock price is higher than the option's strike price. It's calculated as:
  Intrinsic Value of Call=Current Stock Price−Strike Price\text{Intrinsic Value of Call} = \text{Current Stock Price} - \text{Strike

Price}Intrinsic Value of Call=Current Stock Price−Strike Price

If the current stock price is $55 and the call option's strike price is $50, the intrinsic value is $5. If the stock price were below the strike price (e.g., at $45), the intrinsic value would be zero.

- **Put Option Intrinsic Value**: For a put option, intrinsic value exists when the current stock price is lower than the strike price. It's calculated as: Intrinsic Value of Put=Strike Price−Current Stock Price\text{Intrinsic Value of Put} = \text{Strike Price} - \text{Current Stock Price}Intrinsic Value of Put=Strike Price−Current Stock Price

So, if a put option has a strike price of $60 and the current stock price is $55, the intrinsic value is $5.

Note: Intrinsic value cannot be negative. If a call option is "out of the money" (strike price higher than the stock price) or a put option is "out of the money" (strike price lower than the stock price), the intrinsic value is zero. In these cases, the option only has extrinsic value.

Importance of Intrinsic Value in Trading Strategy

The intrinsic value is critical in evaluating an option's profitability at expiration and helps traders determine if an option is "in the money" or "out of the money." Options with intrinsic value may cost more in premiums, but they offer the advantage of immediate value, making them suitable for traders looking for a safer or lower-risk entry point in the market.

2. Extrinsic Value: The Time and Volatility Premium

Extrinsic value, also called **time value**, represents the portion of the option's price that exceeds the intrinsic value. This value is derived from factors such as time until expiration, implied volatility, and the current demand for the option.

Time Value

The **time value** component of an option reflects the amount of time remaining until the option's expiration. Longer timeframes generally result in higher premiums due to increased opportunity for the underlying asset's price to move in a favorable direction.

- **Decay of Time Value**: As an option nears its expiration, the time value diminishes, a phenomenon known as **time decay** or **theta decay**. The time decay accelerates as expiration approaches, meaning options lose value more rapidly in the final days.

Implied Volatility and Market Sentiment

Implied volatility (IV) is a measure of expected price fluctuation in the underlying asset and has a significant impact on the extrinsic value of an option. Higher volatility suggests a greater likelihood of large price swings, which can increase the premium as investors expect a higher chance of achieving intrinsic value before expiration.

- **Impact of Volatility on Options Pricing**: When market conditions are volatile, options premiums tend to rise. Options on high-volatility assets or in uncertain markets carry higher extrinsic value as the potential for profit increases.

Demand and Liquidity

Demand also affects extrinsic value. Highly liquid options, like those for large-cap stocks, tend to have lower spreads between the bid and ask price, making them cheaper to trade. In contrast, less liquid options or those with fewer traders will often be priced higher to offset the greater risk of holding less liquid positions.

3. Time Decay: How Options Lose Value Over Time

Time decay is a natural feature of options that reflects the loss of extrinsic value as the option approaches expiration. As time passes, the probability of the option reaching its strike price decreases, which reduces its market value.

The Concept of Theta

Theta is the Greek term for time decay, representing how much value an option loses each day. For example, if an option has a theta of -0.05, it will lose $0.05 in value every day, assuming other factors remain constant.

- **Accelerating Time Decay**: Time decay is not linear. The impact of theta accelerates as the expiration date nears. Traders must account for this acceleration, as options with high theta values can lose value quickly, especially in the final days of the contract.

Strategic Implications of Time Decay

Understanding time decay can be beneficial in strategies like selling options, where traders aim to profit from the rapid decline in extrinsic value. However, it also poses a risk for options buyers who may find their investments losing value even if the underlying asset performs as expected.

4. Implied Volatility: Expectations for Future Price Movement

Implied volatility (IV) reflects the market's forecast of the future volatility of the underlying asset and plays a central role in options pricing. High implied volatility can significantly increase options premiums, while low implied volatility can lead to lower premiums.

Calculating and Interpreting Implied Volatility

Implied volatility is typically expressed as an annualized percentage and can be derived using the Black-Scholes model or other pricing models. A higher implied volatility indicates a higher chance of price fluctuation, resulting in higher premiums, as traders may see more potential for profitable movements in the stock.

The Volatility Skew

In some cases, options at different strike prices can display varying implied volatility, a concept known as the **volatility skew**. Skews can signal shifts in market sentiment. For instance, a higher implied volatility in put options compared to calls may indicate investor concern about a potential price drop.

Impact on Options Trading Strategies

Traders often monitor implied volatility to gauge when options may be under or overvalued. When IV is high, selling options can be advantageous as they are priced higher. Conversely, buying options in low-IV periods may be beneficial if IV is expected to rise, increasing the option's value.

Understanding options pricing requires balancing intrinsic and extrinsic value, time decay, and implied volatility. Each of these factors offers insights into the potential profitability or risk of an options contract. By evaluating how these elements interact, traders can better gauge the fair value of an option, decide when it is favorable to buy or sell, and anticipate how an option's value may change over time.

In this chapter, we've established a foundational understanding of how options are priced, covering intrinsic and extrinsic value, time decay, and the role of implied volatility. With these concepts, beginners can more confidently analyze and select options that align with their financial goals and risk tolerance. Each section introduces concepts that serve as building blocks for the strategies, risks, and potential returns that follow in options trading, setting the stage for more advanced insights and practices.

Chapter 5

Key Options Trading Strategies for Beginners

Options trading can open a world of financial opportunities and flexibility for investors who seek more than the traditional buy-and-hold strategy. This chapter is dedicated to introducing fundamental options trading strategies ideal for beginners, focusing on methods like buying calls and puts, covered calls, and protective puts. These strategies provide a solid foundation for understanding how options can be used to leverage positions, hedge against losses, or profit from market movements. Before diving into advanced techniques, it's essential to grasp the basics, and this chapter will guide you through each approach with clear explanations and practical examples.

Options strategies can be complex, but by breaking down these beginner-friendly approaches, we can clarify how they work, the risks involved, and the situations where each is most effective. Let's start by exploring the foundational elements of each strategy, discussing key terms, and addressing any potential risks involved.

The Purpose of Options Trading Strategies

When trading options, it's not enough to simply understand how they function; knowing the strategic purposes behind these trades is equally vital. Each options strategy serves a specific function, whether it's to hedge against risk, generate income, or leverage a position for potential gain. Here's an overview of why traders employ these strategies:

1. **Income Generation**: Many options strategies, like the covered call, are used to generate additional income. Investors can benefit from price movements or even neutral trends by collecting premiums, creating a steady cash flow while holding their investments.
2. **Risk Management**: Options provide a valuable tool for hedging against possible losses. Protective puts, for example, can help safeguard an investor's portfolio during times of increased market volatility or downturns.
3. **Speculation**: Options are often used by traders to speculate on the future price of an asset. Buying calls and puts allows investors to take positions that profit from upward or downward movements in stock prices.

4. **Leverage**: Options allow investors to control a larger amount of stock with a relatively smaller amount of capital, offering the potential for amplified returns—albeit with heightened risk.

Understanding why you might choose a particular strategy is crucial before diving into specific methods. Now, let's break down each strategy to understand its mechanics, advantages, and the situations in which it's most appropriate.

Buying Calls: Profiting from an Anticipated Rise in Stock Price

What is a Call Option?

A call option gives the buyer the right, but not the obligation, to purchase a stock at a specified strike price within a certain period. This strategy is appealing to investors who expect the stock price to rise. When the price moves above the strike price, the option holder can exercise the option, buying the asset below the market rate.

Key Characteristics of Buying Calls:

- **Leverage**: A small premium payment provides the potential for significant gains if the stock price rises.
- **Limited Loss Potential**: Loss is capped at the premium paid if the stock doesn't reach the strike price.
- **Profit from Rising Prices**: This strategy is optimal when there's a strong expectation of a price increase in the underlying asset.

Example Scenario:
Imagine a stock currently trading at $50. An investor believes the stock price will increase within the next few months and purchases a call option with a strike price of $55, expiring in three months. If the stock price rises to $60, the option gains value, and the investor has the opportunity to buy the stock at the $55 strike price, potentially profiting from the difference between the market and strike prices minus the premium.

Risks Involved: While buying calls has a lower risk compared to other strategies (as the maximum loss is the premium paid), it's still speculative. If the stock doesn't rise above the strike price, the call will expire worthless, resulting in a total loss of the premium.

Buying Puts: Gaining from a Predicted Decline in Stock Price

What is a Put Option?
A put option grants the buyer the right to sell a stock at a specified strike price within a set period. This strategy is suitable for investors who anticipate a decline in stock price. By purchasing a put, an investor can sell the asset at the strike price even if the market value drops.

Key Characteristics of Buying Puts:

- **Profit from Falling Prices**: Buying a put can be highly profitable if the stock price declines significantly.
- **Hedging Potential**: This strategy also provides a form of insurance for long positions, allowing investors to limit losses.
- **Limited Loss Potential**: As with calls, losses are limited to the premium paid.

Example Scenario:
Consider an investor who owns shares of a company currently valued at $70. The investor anticipates a potential decline due to upcoming market changes, so they buy a put option with a $65 strike price. If the stock drops to $60, the put option allows the investor to sell at $65, mitigating the loss in the stock's value.

Risks Involved: The primary risk when buying puts is that the stock price might not decline as expected, causing the option to expire worthless. In such cases, the investor's loss is limited to the premium paid.

Covered Calls: Generating Income on Owned Stocks

What is a Covered Call?

In a covered call strategy, an investor who owns a stock sells a call option on that stock. This strategy allows the investor to collect a premium from selling the option, which can provide additional income while holding the asset. However, if the stock price exceeds the strike price, the buyer of the call can exercise the option, meaning the investor must sell their shares at the strike price.

Key Characteristics of Covered Calls:

- **Income Generation**: Covered calls are commonly used to generate steady income from stocks an investor already owns.
- **Limited Risk**: Since the investor owns the underlying stock, they're not exposed to the same level of risk as uncovered options.

- **Potential for Partial Gains**: The strategy caps potential gains if the stock price rises above the strike price.

Example Scenario:
An investor owns 100 shares of a company valued at $50 per share. They sell a call option with a $55 strike price, collecting a premium. If the stock stays below $55, the investor keeps both the shares and the premium. If the stock rises above $55, they sell the shares at the strike price but still benefit from the premium and the appreciation up to the strike price.

Risks Involved: The main risk is that if the stock's price surges, the investor must sell their shares at the strike price, potentially missing out on further gains. However, this strategy provides a relatively low-risk way to generate income.

Protective Puts: Hedging Against Potential Losses

What is a Protective Put?
A protective put is essentially an insurance strategy for investors. By buying a put option on a stock they already own, an investor can limit potential losses if the stock

price falls. This strategy is useful during periods of market volatility or when the investor seeks downside protection.

Key Characteristics of Protective Puts:

- **Downside Protection**: If the stock price declines, the put option increases in value, offsetting the loss in the stock's value.
- **Retained Ownership**: Investors can benefit from price increases while limiting potential downside.
- **Cost of Premium**: The main expense for this protection is the premium paid for the put option.

Example Scenario:
An investor holds 200 shares of a stock trading at $40. To protect against a possible downturn, they buy a put option with a $35 strike price. If the stock drops to $30, the put option enables the investor to sell at $35, mitigating the impact of the loss.

Risks Involved: The primary drawback of protective puts is the premium cost, which can add up if used repeatedly. However, this expense can be worth it for investors prioritizing risk management.

When to Use Each Strategy

Understanding when and why to use each strategy is critical for successful options trading. Here's a quick guide to choosing the right approach based on market expectations:

- **Buying Calls**: Best when you anticipate a stock will rise substantially.
- **Buying Puts**: Ideal when expecting a significant decline in stock price.
- **Covered Calls**: Useful for generating income on stocks you already own without expecting large price jumps.
- **Protective Puts**: Perfect for investors who want to hold stocks but need a safeguard against a possible downturn.

Chapter 6

Risk Management in Options Trading

Options trading, while potentially profitable, comes with its share of risks. Because of the leveraged nature of options, a trader can either magnify gains or experience substantial losses quickly. This dual potential underscores the importance of **risk management** as a core skill in options trading. In this chapter, we will explore several essential methods for managing and mitigating risks, ensuring that traders are prepared not only to capitalize on profitable trades but also to protect their portfolios from unexpected losses.

The chapter will cover practical approaches to managing risk, including the use of stop-loss orders, position sizing, and hedging techniques. It will also address safety precautions, regulatory considerations, and emphasize the importance of a disciplined approach to options trading. With a clear understanding of these strategies, beginner and intermediate traders alike can make informed decisions that help them stay in the game longer, even through market volatility.

Understanding Risk in Options Trading

The Nature of Options Risk

Options trading is inherently riskier than traditional stock investing because of its potential for high leverage. Leverage allows traders to control large amounts of stock with a relatively small amount of capital. However, with this leverage comes the possibility of rapid losses if the market does not move in the anticipated direction. The potential to lose the entire amount invested in an option contract—known as **total loss exposure**—highlights the need for effective risk management strategies.

Options trading also involves complex factors like time decay (the loss of value as an option approaches expiration), volatility, and market movements that can quickly erode gains. Without proper risk management, even a well-researched options strategy can lead to substantial financial setbacks.

Key Risks in Options Trading

Understanding the specific risks associated with options trading is crucial for effective risk management. Here are some of the core risks to consider:

- **Market Risk**: Market risk is the risk of losing money due to fluctuations in the price of the underlying asset. This is a key risk factor, especially for options buyers, as price movements directly affect the value of options contracts.
- **Time Decay**: For most options contracts, value diminishes as expiration approaches, a concept known as **theta decay** or time decay. This affects especially short-term options holders who must be precise in timing their trades to avoid a significant drop in value.
- **Volatility Risk**: Options prices are sensitive to changes in the volatility of the underlying asset. A sudden drop in volatility, often measured as **implied volatility**, can lead to a decrease in the option's premium, even if the underlying asset's price remains stable.
- **Liquidity Risk**: For certain options, finding a willing buyer or seller at the desired price can be difficult, leading to **liquidity risk**. This is especially common in options with a low trading volume and can lead to challenges in entering or exiting positions at favorable prices.

Stop-Loss Orders: Limiting Potential Losses

What Are Stop-Loss Orders?

A **stop-loss order** is a pre-set order to sell a security once it reaches a specific price, intended to limit an investor's loss on a position. This is an essential tool for managing risks, as it creates a safety net that minimizes the chance of enduring substantial losses. While commonly used in stock trading, stop-loss orders are just as effective in options trading, allowing traders to control the downside on their investments.

Types of Stop-Loss Orders

- **Standard Stop-Loss**: Triggers a market order to sell the option at the next available price once the price drops to a certain level. While effective, this can sometimes result in a lower-than-expected sale price, particularly in volatile markets.
- **Trailing Stop-Loss**: Adjusts the stop price at a fixed percentage below the option's market price, allowing for flexibility and letting traders capture gains if the price rises.

Setting Stop-Loss Levels for Options

Setting an appropriate stop-loss level is crucial. The level should neither be so close that normal fluctuations trigger a sell-off, nor so far away that losses become unmanageable. A typical guideline is to set a stop-loss level based on a percentage of the option premium or the value of the underlying asset. For example, if an option premium is $10, a stop-loss at $8 could cap losses at a manageable level while allowing for normal fluctuations.

In options trading, stop-loss orders are also helpful for traders who prefer to **write options**, as they can help limit losses if the market moves unexpectedly against the option writer.

Position Sizing: Managing Exposure

Importance of Position Sizing

Position sizing is the process of determining the amount of capital to allocate to each trade, a foundational principle in managing trading risk. In options trading, proper position sizing helps mitigate the risk of significant losses and protects the trader's overall portfolio. By carefully choosing the size of each position, traders can control their level of exposure and avoid over-committing to a single trade, which can be particularly dangerous in the volatile options market.

Guidelines for Effective Position Sizing

- **Percentage of Portfolio**: A common rule is to risk only a small percentage of the total portfolio on each options trade, typically no more than 1-5%. This approach limits the potential impact of a loss on any single trade.
- **Risk per Trade**: Another approach involves calculating risk based on a dollar amount that aligns with the trader's tolerance. For example, if a trader is willing to risk $200 per trade, they can use this amount to determine the number of options contracts to buy or sell.
- **Volatility Considerations**: In volatile markets, reducing position size can be an effective way to limit risk. Higher volatility means a greater chance of the underlying asset moving unexpectedly, making smaller positions more manageable.

Position Sizing and Leverage

Options inherently provide leverage, which can amplify both gains and losses. Leverage should be used with caution, and understanding the extent of leverage in a trade is crucial for managing risk. Many traders adopt a

conservative approach to leverage, using only a portion of available buying power rather than maximizing it, which minimizes the chance of substantial losses in a downturn.

Hedging Techniques: Reducing Market Exposure

What is Hedging?

Hedging is a risk management strategy that involves taking offsetting positions to reduce the impact of adverse market movements. In options trading, hedging can help traders protect their portfolios from sudden losses by balancing exposure to different market conditions. For example, purchasing put options on a stock can hedge against potential losses if the stock price declines, providing a safety net for the trader's long position.

Popular Hedging Techniques in Options Trading

1. Protective Puts

A **protective put** is an options strategy where an investor holding a long position in a stock buys a put option on the same stock. This way, if the stock price drops, the gains on the put option can help offset losses on the stock. Protective puts are commonly used by traders looking to protect their gains in a volatile market or during uncertain economic conditions.

2. Covered Calls

In a **covered call** strategy, an investor who owns a stock sells call options on that stock to generate income. While it limits the upside potential of the stock, it provides some downside protection. The premium earned from selling the call option helps offset any losses if the stock price falls.

3. Spreads

Options spreads are combinations of two or more options to reduce risk or profit from specific market scenarios. Examples include **bull call spreads**, **bear put spreads**, and **iron condors**. Each type of spread offers a different balance of risk and reward, allowing traders to align their strategy with their market outlook and risk tolerance.

Advanced Hedging Techniques

While protective puts, covered calls, and basic spreads form the foundation of hedging in options trading, more advanced hedging strategies can offer nuanced control over risk. These techniques require a solid understanding of options mechanics but can be invaluable for traders looking to tailor their risk management more precisely.

1. Collar Strategy

A **collar strategy** is commonly used by traders who want to protect a long stock position. In this strategy, the trader buys a put option to guard against downside risk while simultaneously selling a call option to generate income. The income from selling the call offsets the cost of the protective put, making this strategy more cost-effective. However, it limits the upside potential of the stock, as the trader is obligated to sell it at the strike price of the call if it is exercised.

- **Example**: If a trader owns shares of a stock trading at $50 and expects it to remain relatively stable, they could buy a put with a $45 strike price to protect against significant losses. At the same time, they might sell a call with a $55 strike price to generate income. This setup limits their maximum loss and gain, creating a controlled risk environment.

2. Long Straddle

The **long straddle** is a strategy where a trader buys both a call and a put option on the same asset with the same strike price and expiration date. This strategy is typically used when a trader anticipates significant volatility but is uncertain about the direction of the move. While this strategy can be costly, as the trader is paying for two premiums, it offers substantial upside if the underlying asset moves significantly.

- **Example**: If a stock is trading at $100 and earnings are approaching, the trader might buy a call and a put option at a $100 strike price. If the stock makes a large move in either direction, the profits from one option could offset the loss of the other and potentially generate a significant net gain.

3. Iron Condor

An **iron condor** is a four-leg options strategy that combines two vertical spreads (a bull put spread and a bear call spread) on the same asset with the same expiration date. This strategy profits from low volatility when the stock price remains within a specific range. By limiting both maximum gains and losses, the iron condor creates a controlled-risk trade, suitable for traders with a neutral outlook.

- **Example**: If a stock is trading at $50, a trader might sell a $55 call and buy a $60 call, while simultaneously selling a $45 put and buying a $40 put. This establishes a range within which the trader profits, as long as the stock price stays between $45 and $55.

Regulatory Considerations in Risk Management

The Role of the SEC and FINRA

When managing risk in options trading, it's essential to understand the **regulatory environment** governing the options market. The **Securities and Exchange Commission (SEC)** and the **Financial Industry Regulatory Authority (FINRA)** regulate options trading in the United States. They oversee practices to ensure market stability and protect traders, particularly retail investors.

These agencies set guidelines that brokers must follow, such as enforcing margin requirements, maintaining appropriate disclosures, and preventing excessive risk-taking by retail investors. FINRA also categorizes options into different levels, with higher-risk strategies like spreads and naked options only available to more experienced investors.

Regulatory Guidelines on Position Sizing and Leverage

Brokers are legally obligated to ensure that their clients trade within certain limits based on their financial standing, experience, and risk tolerance. For example:

- **Margin Requirements**: Brokers enforce margin requirements on specific options strategies, especially those that carry higher risk, such as uncovered calls. These requirements are designed to ensure that investors have sufficient capital to cover potential losses.
- **Suitability Standards**: Under FINRA's "Know Your Customer" rule, brokers must assess a trader's experience and financial situation to determine suitability for complex strategies. This rule protects inexperienced traders from entering positions that could lead to substantial losses.

Legal Disclosures and Risk Warnings

Options trading platforms are required to provide disclosures that outline the risks involved, including the **Options Disclosure Document (ODD)**, which all traders must review before trading. This document covers the mechanics of options, associated risks, and explains strategies that may result in substantial losses. Reading the ODD is essential, as it provides a realistic view of potential risks in options trading.

Psychological Aspects of Risk Management

The Role of Emotion in Options Trading

Successful risk management requires more than technical knowledge; it also involves the ability to remain calm and objective under pressure. **Emotional discipline** is critical in options trading, as market volatility and unexpected outcomes can lead to impulsive decisions. Traders who cannot manage their emotions effectively are more likely to deviate from their planned risk management strategies, increasing the likelihood of significant losses.

Strategies for Maintaining Discipline

1. **Setting Clear Rules**: Creating rules for each trade, such as setting stop-loss limits and position size, can reduce impulsive decisions. These rules should be part of a well-structured trading plan that the trader adheres to consistently.
2. **Practicing Patience**: Emotional control is often tested by the urge to exit a position too early or enter a position too late. Practicing patience and waiting for ideal setups helps traders avoid high-risk, low-reward trades driven by impatience.
3. **Keeping a Trading Journal**: Documenting each trade, including the rationale, emotions, and outcomes, allows traders to review and learn from their experiences. Over time, this helps build emotional resilience and refine risk management strategies.

Practical Tips for Effective Risk Management

Here are some practical tips that can help traders improve their risk management approach:

1. **Focus on Capital Preservation**: Protecting capital should be a top priority. This means not risking too much on a single trade and employing conservative position sizing techniques.
2. **Stay Informed**: Keep up with market news, economic events, and any factors that may influence volatility. This knowledge can help traders make informed decisions about risk exposure.
3. **Review and Adjust Strategies Regularly**: The market is dynamic, and risk management strategies should evolve accordingly. Regularly reviewing strategies and adjusting them to match current market conditions is crucial for long-term success.
4. **Use Technology to Assist**: Many brokerage platforms offer risk management tools, such as alerts, automated stop-loss orders, and volatility indicators. Leveraging these tools can make managing risk more effective and less time-consuming.

Chapter 7

Reading Options Chains and Market Indicators

When starting with options trading, one of the first and most essential skills to develop is understanding options chains and how to interpret them. Options chains are listings of all available options for a given underlying asset, organized by expiry date, strike price, and other important data points. They contain a wealth of information for traders, helping to gauge the market's perspective on an asset's future price and volatility. In this chapter, we'll break down the various components of an options chain, explain key concepts like bid-ask spreads, and introduce useful market indicators that can help identify trading opportunities.

Understanding these elements isn't just about knowledge; it's about gaining the tools to make informed trading decisions. With the information laid out in this chapter, you'll be well on your way to understanding options chains, finding profitable strategies, and navigating the options market more confidently.

Introduction to Options Chains

Options chains are like the language of options trading. Each row and column in an options chain conveys critical information, from pricing to market interest, that allows traders to form educated guesses about the likely future of an underlying asset. Unlike regular stocks, which have one price at any given time, options have multiple possible outcomes due to factors like strike price, expiration, and volatility. This complexity is what gives options their versatility—and also what makes understanding options chains so important.

Reading an options chain is about more than understanding the numbers; it's about interpreting the sentiment and predictions of other market participants. The data in an options chain represents the aggregate view of traders on an asset's likely path, allowing individuals to align their trades accordingly. Throughout this chapter, we'll build up this skill step-by-step, so each aspect of the options chain becomes familiar territory.

Components of an Options Chain

Strike Price

The **strike price** is the predetermined price at which an option can be exercised. For call options, this is the price at which the holder has the right to buy the asset, while for put options, it's the price at which the holder has the right to sell. Options chains organize contracts by strike price in ascending or descending order, depending on the platform.

Strike price is a key component in determining an option's intrinsic value—whether or not an option has any real worth in its current state. Options are classified as:

- **In-the-money (ITM)**: When exercising the option would result in a profit.
- **At-the-money (ATM)**: When the asset price is approximately equal to the strike price.
- **Out-of-the-money (OTM)**: When exercising the option would not result in a profit.

Understanding how different strike prices affect potential profit or loss is essential. Traders often use strike price as a reference to set up strategies based on where they believe the market is headed.

Expiry Date

Options contracts have **expiry dates**, marking the last day the contract can be exercised. Options chains often group options by their expiration, and traders typically see monthly or weekly expiration dates available. Expiry dates impact an option's time decay and are crucial for deciding when to buy or sell.

- **Near-term expirations** tend to have lower premiums and are impacted more quickly by time decay, also known as **theta**.
- **Longer-term expirations** provide more time for the option to move into profitability but usually come with higher premiums due to the additional time value.

Different strategies cater to different expiration windows. Some traders might buy options with short expirations if they anticipate an immediate move, while others might prefer long-term options, known as **LEAPS** (Long-Term Equity Anticipation Securities), for a more extended investment outlook.

Open Interest and Volume

Open interest reflects the total number of open positions, either bought or sold, on a particular options contract. High open interest often indicates a popular strike or expiry date and suggests that many traders are interested in this particular price level. **Volume**, on the other hand, shows the number of contracts traded during a specific period, usually one day. While volume reflects daily activity, open interest provides insight into how many contracts are active in total.

Volume and open interest are used together to gauge market sentiment:

- High volume and open interest suggest strong trader interest.
- Low volume and high open interest might suggest reluctance to trade despite holding positions.
- High volume with low open interest could indicate positions closing out.

Using open interest and volume data, traders can make informed predictions on how a particular option is likely to perform.

Interpreting Bid-Ask Spreads

The **bid-ask spread** is a critical concept in understanding the pricing of options. The **bid price** is what buyers are willing to pay, while the **ask price** is what sellers are asking for the option. The difference between these two prices is the **spread**, which represents the market's liquidity and cost of entry.

In general:

- Narrow spreads indicate a liquid market with many participants.
- Wide spreads indicate a less liquid market, where buying and selling are less frequent.

When the bid-ask spread is wide, it might be more challenging for traders to execute trades at favorable prices, potentially affecting profitability. New traders should aim for liquid options with narrow spreads to minimize trading costs and ease entry and exit from positions.

Factors that affect the bid-ask spread include:

- **Underlying asset volatility**: More volatile assets usually have wider spreads.
- **Trading volume**: Higher volume can lead to tighter spreads.
- **Time to expiration**: As expiration nears, spreads may narrow due to increased trading activity.

Learning to assess spreads is vital for recognizing the hidden costs in options trading and can help beginners choose trades that offer favorable entry and exit points.

Key Market Indicators for Options Trading

While options chains provide the essential details of each contract, market indicators allow traders to assess potential profitability and risk. Understanding these indicators helps traders identify opportunities and make informed choices. Here are some of the most commonly used indicators in options trading.

Implied Volatility

Implied volatility (IV) reflects the market's forecast of a stock's future volatility and is a crucial part of options pricing. Higher IV suggests the market anticipates large price movements, which generally increases options premiums. Low IV indicates a calmer market and lower premiums.

- **High IV** may suggest potential for larger price swings, making options more expensive.
- **Low IV** can make options cheaper, but with potentially less movement.

IV is often displayed on an options chain, giving traders insight into the market's sentiment on future volatility. Understanding IV can also help in choosing the right strategy—higher IV may favor strategies like straddles, while lower IV might benefit strategies like covered calls.

The Greeks

The **Greeks**—delta, gamma, theta, vega, and rho—are indicators that help traders understand how options prices are affected by various factors.

- **Delta**: Measures the option's sensitivity to price changes in the underlying asset.
- **Gamma**: Represents the rate of change in delta.
- **Theta**: Reflects time decay, the loss in value as expiration nears.
- **Vega**: Shows the option's sensitivity to volatility.
- **Rho**: Indicates sensitivity to interest rate changes.

By using the Greeks, traders can get a clearer sense of the risks associated with different positions. Each Greek measures a specific risk factor, making them powerful tools for adjusting positions according to market conditions.

Practical Example of Reading an Options Chain

Let's apply the information from this chapter to analyze a sample options chain for a hypothetical stock, "XYZ Corp." Consider various expiry dates, strike prices, open interest, and IV levels to demonstrate how a trader might read an options chain and select a trade that fits their outlook and risk tolerance.

Legal and Risk Considerations

Options trading carries significant risk, and understanding these risks is essential for every trader. Contracts may expire worthless, leading to a complete loss of the premium paid. Regulatory bodies like the SEC provide guidelines on options trading, emphasizing the importance of understanding and managing risk.

Before trading, new options traders are advised to:

- Ensure they meet their brokerage's suitability requirements for options trading.
- Start with paper trading or a simulation to practice without risking real capital.

- Understand their legal obligations, such as taxes on options gains.

Chapter 8

Options Expiration and Assignment

Options expiration and assignment are crucial aspects of options trading that can significantly impact a trader's strategy and position outcomes. This chapter explores the expiration process, details the assignment mechanism, and examines how each can affect an options trader's portfolio. Understanding these concepts is essential for managing risk, planning trade exits, and optimizing profits. Knowing how expiration and assignment work can also help traders avoid unwanted outcomes, such as unexpected stock purchases or sales.

Introduction to Options Expiration and Assignment

Options trading brings a level of flexibility not found in standard stock trades, but with this flexibility comes complexity. At the core of options trading are two pivotal events: expiration and assignment. Each has unique rules, timelines, and consequences that affect every options contract. **Expiration** is the date when an options contract becomes invalid, determining whether the option is exercised or expires worthless. **Assignment** happens when an options seller is required to fulfill the contract terms if the option is exercised by the holder.

While both concepts are fundamental, they often confuse beginner traders. This chapter clarifies how expiration and assignment work, why they matter, and how traders can navigate them to enhance strategy effectiveness and risk management.

Options Expiration: Key Concepts

Expiration is the final day an options contract is valid. By this date, the holder must decide whether to exercise the option, sell it, or let it expire. Each choice has unique consequences and is influenced by the option's intrinsic value, time decay, and market volatility.

Expiration Dates

The **expiration date** is the date on which an option contract becomes invalid. It usually falls on the third Friday of the expiration month for monthly options, but weekly and quarterly options may expire on different dates. Knowing when an option expires is critical because it marks the last opportunity for the holder to exercise it.

- **Monthly Expirations:** The majority of stock options expire on the third Friday of the expiration month. This is standard for many contracts, making it easy for traders to track.
- **Weekly Expirations:** Many stocks also offer weekly options, which expire every Friday. Weekly expirations provide additional flexibility for short-term strategies, allowing traders to take advantage of market fluctuations within a shorter timeframe.
- **Quarterly Expirations:** These options expire on the last business day of each quarter and are often used by institutional investors and traders with longer-term strategies.

Options Cycles and Expiry Calendar

Understanding **options cycles** is another part of managing options expiration. An options cycle indicates the months in which specific contracts expire, and each option belongs to one of three cycles:

1. **Cycle 1:** January, April, July, and October
2. **Cycle 2:** February, May, August, and November
3. **Cycle 3:** March, June, September, and December

With these cycles, traders can plan trades around expiration patterns and select contracts that align with their timing needs.

Expiration Implications for Different Options Strategies

The impact of expiration varies based on the type of options strategy used. Here's a look at how expiration affects some common strategies:

- **Long Calls and Puts:** For long calls and puts, expiration is critical because the option will expire worthless if it is out of the money (OTM) at the expiration date. The trader must assess whether the potential reward justifies the risk of the premium paid.
- **Covered Calls:** Expiration can be a favorable event in covered call strategies, particularly if the option expires out of the money. When this occurs, the trader keeps the premium without having to sell the underlying asset, allowing for further income generation.
- **Protective Puts:** Protective puts serve as insurance on long stock positions. If the stock price drops below the strike price at expiration, the put provides downside protection. However, if the stock price remains above the strike price, the option expires worthless, and the trader incurs the cost of the premium.

Understanding the role of expiration in each strategy is essential to optimize returns and reduce risks.

Assignment Process: How It Works

Assignment occurs when the holder of an options contract decides to exercise it, and the seller (writer) is obligated to fulfill the contract terms. For options writers, assignment can happen any time after the sale of the contract, which is why it's important to be prepared for potential obligations.

Understanding Exercise and Assignment

- **Exercise:** When the holder exercises an option, they enforce the terms of the contract. In the case of a call option, they buy the underlying asset at the strike price. With a put option, they sell the asset at the strike price.
- **Assignment:** For the writer, assignment means they are required to fulfill the contract terms. This process is automatic in most markets and handled by the broker.

Assignment can be unpredictable for sellers, as it depends on the buyer's decision to exercise. Typically, options that are in the money (ITM) near expiration are most likely to be exercised, resulting in assignment.

The Role of Brokers in Assignment

Brokers facilitate the assignment process, ensuring that both the buyer's and the seller's obligations are met seamlessly. The Options Clearing Corporation (OCC) standardizes and regulates assignment processes, reducing the risk for both parties involved.

Brokers follow a random assignment process for option writers, meaning that anyone with an open short position can be assigned when the option is exercised by the holder. While this system is designed to be fair, traders should still be prepared for the financial and logistical requirements of assignment, particularly for short options.

Risks and Considerations in Assignment

Assignment can have various financial and tax implications. Being assigned requires either delivering the underlying asset (for calls) or buying it (for puts), which may incur significant costs. Therefore, traders should have a clear understanding of how assignment aligns with their broader portfolio and financial plans.

Potential Impacts on Your Options Positions

Understanding the effects of expiration and assignment is essential for successful options trading, as each event brings unique challenges and opportunities.

Effects on Call and Put Options

When options reach expiration, they either expire worthless, are exercised, or are automatically assigned if they are in the money. For long options, expiration without exercise results in the loss of the premium. For options that are in the money, automatic exercise or assignment can occur based on the broker's policies and the option's value relative to the strike price.

Strategies to Manage Expiring Options

To manage options approaching expiration, traders use several strategies:

- **Rolling Options:** Rolling involves closing the current position and opening a new one with a later expiration. This can help in extending the trade and preserving the strategy if the option has potential to gain value.
- **Close or Offset the Position:** Traders often close positions near expiration to avoid assignment,

particularly if the underlying stock could make an unwanted move. Closing the position helps lock in profits or reduce potential losses.
- **Letting Options Expire:** In some cases, letting an option expire worthless can be the most cost-effective choice. This approach is common when the option is far out of the money, and the cost of closing the position would exceed any potential gain.

Tax Implications and Reporting Requirements

The tax consequences of expiration and assignment vary by country and account type, such as individual or retirement accounts. In general:

- **Expired Options:** Expired options typically result in a capital loss for the holder. Reporting requirements may depend on whether the options were part of a strategy, such as a covered call or protective put.
- **Assignment:** When assigned, the cost basis of the underlying asset may change, which has implications for both short-term and long-term capital gains calculations.

Consulting a tax professional or financial advisor is advisable to manage these complex tax reporting obligations effectively.

Chapter 9

The Role of Volatility in Options Trading

Understanding volatility is central to effective options trading. Volatility doesn't just influence price movement; it directly impacts the profitability and risk of options strategies. For both novice and experienced traders, being able to interpret and capitalize on volatility is a powerful skill that enables informed decision-making and the optimization of trading strategies.

This chapter explores the concept of volatility in depth—how it's calculated, how to interpret it, and, importantly, how traders can leverage it. We'll cover essential volatility-based strategies like straddles and strangles, examining their potential for profit and discussing how to mitigate the risks involved. We'll also touch on the role of implied volatility and its relationship to market sentiment.

Understanding Volatility in Options Trading

What Is Volatility?

In the context of financial markets, **volatility** refers to the extent of price fluctuations in an asset over a specific period. When the price of a stock, index, or other asset swings dramatically up and down, it's considered highly volatile. Conversely, when prices are relatively stable, the asset is seen as having low volatility.

In options trading, volatility is crucial because it affects the premium—or price—of an option. Options tied to highly volatile assets generally have higher premiums, reflecting the increased uncertainty and risk. There are two main types of volatility relevant to options traders: historical volatility and implied volatility.

Historical Volatility vs. Implied Volatility

Historical Volatility

Historical volatility (HV) is a backward-looking measure that shows how much the price of an asset has fluctuated over a certain period. Calculated using past price data, historical volatility can help traders understand an asset's typical behavior. High historical volatility suggests that the asset's price has been more variable, while low historical volatility indicates steadier price movement.

For example, if a stock's price has fluctuated significantly over the past year, it will have high historical volatility. Knowing an asset's historical volatility can give traders context about what to expect, although it's not a guarantee of future performance.

Implied Volatility

Implied volatility (IV) is a forward-looking metric that reflects market expectations about an asset's future volatility. Unlike historical volatility, which is derived from past prices, implied volatility is calculated based on current option prices, making it a critical component in the options pricing model (typically the Black-Scholes model).

Higher implied volatility means traders expect more significant price movements, either up or down, in the future. Conversely, lower implied volatility suggests expectations of relatively stable prices. IV tends to rise during times of uncertainty or anticipated market events, such as earnings announcements, economic data releases, or geopolitical events.

Since IV directly affects option premiums, a higher IV increases the cost of options, while a lower IV reduces it.

As a result, many traders monitor IV closely to identify potentially profitable trading opportunities and to gauge market sentiment.

The Impact of Volatility on Option Pricing

The Options Pricing Model and Volatility

In options trading, pricing models like the Black-Scholes formula factor in volatility when calculating an option's premium. Volatility is one of the main "Greeks," a set of variables that affect an option's price, alongside others like delta and theta. Specifically, **Vega** is the Greek representing an option's sensitivity to volatility.

- **Vega and Option Price Sensitivity**: When Vega is high, an option's price will be more sensitive to changes in volatility. For instance, a rise in implied volatility will increase the value of both call and put options, making them more expensive to buy but potentially more profitable to sell.

Volatility's Effect on Different Strategies

Because volatility influences option prices, it has a direct impact on the potential profitability of various options strategies. For example:

- **Long Options**: Buying calls or puts benefits from rising implied volatility, as this increases the value of the position.
- **Short Options**: Selling options, conversely, may benefit from falling volatility, as a decrease in IV reduces the option premium and, therefore, the potential liability of the seller.

The relationship between volatility and strategy can be complex, so let's dive into some common volatility-based options strategies and how they work in practice.

Volatility-Based Strategies: Straddles, Strangles, and More

When volatility is expected to increase or is currently high, certain strategies can help traders benefit from potential price swings in either direction. Here, we explore some key strategies that leverage volatility.

The Straddle: Profiting from Uncertainty

A **straddle** involves buying a call option and a put option at the same strike price and expiration date. This strategy allows the trader to profit regardless of the direction in which the asset moves, as long as the movement is significant enough to offset the combined cost of both options.

How a Straddle Works

In a straddle, the two options (call and put) work together to create a position that is "direction-neutral." Whether the price rises or falls, the trader stands to make a profit if the movement is large enough. However, the strategy's effectiveness depends heavily on volatility. If the market remains relatively stable, the straddle may result in a loss because the option premiums will decay over time.

When to Use a Straddle

A straddle can be particularly effective when volatility is expected to spike due to an upcoming event, such as:

- **Earnings Announcements**: Earnings releases can cause significant stock price movements.
- **Product Launches or Corporate Announcements**: Major announcements often create uncertainty and large price fluctuations.

- **Economic Data Releases**: News on interest rates, employment figures, or inflation data can impact market volatility.

Since implied volatility tends to rise before these events, the cost of entering a straddle may also be higher. Traders must weigh the potential gain against this increased cost.

The Strangle: A More Cost-Effective Approach

A **strangle** is similar to a straddle but involves buying out-of-the-money call and put options with the same expiration date but different strike prices. This strategy is generally cheaper than a straddle because the options are further from the current market price, making them less expensive.

How a Strangle Works

In a strangle, the trader profits if the asset moves significantly in either direction. The advantage of the strangle is its lower cost compared to a straddle, as the options are out-of-the-money. However, this also means the price movement must be more substantial to reach profitability.

When to Use a Strangle

A strangle is best used in situations where a trader expects significant volatility but wants to reduce upfront costs. Like a straddle, strangles are useful before anticipated events but may also be employed in markets that are generally volatile or unpredictable.

Using Market Indicators to Predict Volatility

In addition to the Greeks, several market indicators can help traders gauge expected volatility and decide when to employ volatility-based strategies.

Volatility Index (VIX)

The **Volatility Index (VIX)**, often referred to as the "fear index," measures the implied volatility of S&P 500 index options. A higher VIX reading indicates that the market anticipates larger-than-normal price movements, while a lower VIX suggests expectations of stability.

Many traders use the VIX as a general barometer for market sentiment and volatility trends. When the VIX is high, strategies that capitalize on large price swings, such as straddles and strangles, may be more attractive. Conversely, a low VIX might make strategies that benefit from stability, like selling covered calls, more appealing.

Moving Averages and Standard Deviation

Moving averages and **standard deviation** are also valuable for understanding volatility. When prices deviate significantly from their moving averages, volatility may increase. Likewise, high standard deviation readings reflect larger price fluctuations.

Bollinger Bands

Bollinger Bands are another helpful indicator. By plotting a moving average with upper and lower bands based on standard deviations, traders can visualize price volatility. A "breakout" beyond these bands may suggest high volatility, whereas trading within the bands indicates relative stability.

Chapter 10

Fundamental Analysis for Options Trading

Fundamental analysis is a key approach for traders seeking to understand and predict the value of an underlying asset. Unlike technical analysis, which examines price patterns and trading volume, fundamental analysis focuses on the "big picture" — the financial health and performance metrics of a company, economic indicators, and broader market trends. This approach can offer a clear view of an asset's intrinsic value, making it particularly valuable in options trading, where timing and anticipation of price movements are crucial.

In options trading, understanding the fundamental drivers of a stock or other underlying asset enables traders to make more informed bets. For example, knowing that a company is on the verge of a major product launch or that the Federal Reserve may adjust interest rates can help traders anticipate shifts in asset prices, potentially improving their strategies and outcomes. However, successful use of fundamental analysis requires knowledge of multiple economic and financial indicators and an understanding of how these metrics can impact market behavior.

This chapter will walk you through the essential aspects of fundamental analysis for options trading, including how to assess company financials, interpret macroeconomic data, and incorporate market sentiment into your trading strategy. You'll learn how these components can inform various options trades and boost the probability of successful outcomes.

Key Components of Fundamental Analysis

Fundamental analysis for options trading involves several core components:

1. Company Financials

A company's financial health is at the heart of its stock's intrinsic value. By evaluating financial statements, traders can understand how a company generates revenue, manages expenses, and handles debt. Key financial documents include the income statement, balance sheet, and cash flow statement. Let's break down each one:

a. Income Statement

The income statement shows the company's revenue, expenses, and net income over a specific period. This document reveals how much profit the company is making and whether that profit is growing, shrinking, or remaining stable.

- **Revenue**: The total income generated from the sale of goods or services. High revenue growth is a good indicator that a company is expanding its market presence or increasing its product sales.
- **Net Income**: Often called the "bottom line," this is the company's total earnings after all expenses are deducted from revenue. Rising net income suggests profitability and efficient cost management, which can lead to stock price appreciation.
- **Earnings Per Share (EPS)**: EPS is calculated by dividing net income by the number of outstanding shares. A growing EPS can indicate improved profitability per share, making the stock more attractive to investors.

b. Balance Sheet

The balance sheet provides a snapshot of the company's financial position at a given point in time, showing its assets, liabilities, and shareholders' equity.

- **Assets**: Assets include both current assets (like cash and receivables) and fixed assets (such as property and equipment). A company with significant assets may have a cushion to weather economic downturns.
- **Liabilities**: Liabilities are the company's debts and obligations. A high debt-to-equity ratio, for instance, can signal financial risk if a company relies too heavily on borrowed money.
- **Shareholders' Equity**: This is the residual interest in the assets of the company after deducting liabilities. It represents the net worth of the company from shareholders' perspective and can indicate growth potential.

c. Cash Flow Statement

The cash flow statement details cash inflows and outflows, focusing on operating, investing, and financing activities.

- **Operating Cash Flow**: Cash flow from operations reflects the company's core business operations. A positive and growing operating cash flow is a sign of a healthy company.
- **Investing and Financing Cash Flow**: These sections indicate where the company is investing its capital and how it is financing growth (e.g., through debt or equity). High levels of

investment may suggest plans for expansion, which can be a bullish indicator.

Understanding these financial metrics can provide insights into a company's stability and growth prospects, helping options traders anticipate price movements. For instance, if a company reports strong earnings growth, it may attract bullish sentiment, raising the stock price and increasing the value of call options on that stock.

---

2. Economic Indicators and Market Conditions

Options trading doesn't happen in a vacuum. Broader economic conditions, such as interest rates, inflation, and employment trends, also impact asset prices. Traders who understand how to read economic indicators can better predict market sentiment and stock movements. Here are some key indicators:

a. Interest Rates

Interest rates influence borrowing costs, consumer spending, and investment decisions. When rates rise, it becomes more expensive for businesses to finance growth, which can dampen stock prices. Conversely, lower interest rates often stimulate economic activity, increasing demand for stocks. For options traders, a rate hike could suggest a bearish outlook on certain sectors, whereas a rate cut could prompt bullish trades.

b. Inflation Rates

High inflation reduces purchasing power, which can lead to lower consumer spending. Inflation can also increase operational costs for companies, impacting their profitability. Inflation data is essential for options traders, as it can signal potential shifts in stock prices and help inform strategies for hedging or speculating on market movement.

c. Unemployment Rates

Unemployment data reflects the health of the labor market. High unemployment can signal economic instability, potentially lowering stock prices, while low unemployment suggests economic strength, boosting investor confidence. Tracking unemployment trends can help traders anticipate market shifts and adjust their positions accordingly.

d. Gross Domestic Product (GDP)

GDP is a measure of the country's overall economic activity. A growing GDP indicates economic expansion, which can boost stock prices, while a contracting GDP may trigger bearish market sentiment. Options traders may use GDP trends to identify bullish or bearish positions depending on economic growth expectations.

Fundamental Analysis Strategies for Options Traders

With a solid understanding of financial and economic indicators, options traders can develop specific strategies based on fundamental analysis. Here are some popular strategies:

1. Earnings-Based Trading Strategies

Companies report earnings quarterly, and these reports often lead to significant stock price volatility. Options traders can use earnings reports to speculate on short-term price movements. Here are a few common earnings-based strategies:

a. Straddle and Strangle

A straddle involves buying both a call and a put option at the same strike price and expiration date. This strategy profits if the stock price moves significantly, regardless of the direction. In contrast, a strangle involves buying a call and put with different strike prices but the same expiration date. Traders often use these strategies before an earnings report, anticipating a price swing.

b. Covered Calls and Protective Puts

A covered call strategy involves holding a stock and selling a call option on it. This approach can generate income if the stock remains relatively stable. On the other hand, a protective put involves holding a stock and buying a put option as a hedge. This limits potential losses if the stock declines following disappointing earnings.

c. Iron Condor

An iron condor strategy combines four options: two calls and two puts with different strike prices but the same expiration. This strategy is ideal when a trader expects minimal price movement after earnings, allowing them to profit from time decay on the options' premium.

Each of these strategies requires an understanding of the potential risks associated with market-moving events like earnings reports. Misinterpreting earnings results or overlooking market sentiment can lead to losses, so careful analysis and risk management are essential.

---

2. Leveraging Economic Events and News

Market-moving events, such as central bank announcements, geopolitical developments, and economic reports, can create opportunities for options trades. Here's how traders can approach these events:

a. Trading on Interest Rate Decisions

Central banks, particularly the Federal Reserve, influence markets through monetary policy changes. If a rate hike is anticipated, traders may consider bearish positions on rate-sensitive sectors like real estate. Conversely, a rate cut may create bullish opportunities in consumer discretionary sectors.

b. Positioning for Geopolitical Events

Geopolitical tensions or trade agreements can impact specific industries. For instance, a major trade agreement may boost the stocks of companies with large export markets, presenting call option opportunities. Conversely, international tensions could create volatility, opening the door for strategies like straddles.

Integrating Market Sentiment into Options Trading

Market sentiment — the overall mood or tone of investors regarding a particular asset or market — plays a critical role in options trading. While market sentiment is often associated with technical analysis, it can also be evaluated through fundamental indicators, such as consumer confidence indexes, company announcements, and macroeconomic trends. For options traders, understanding sentiment can improve the accuracy of trades and help align positions with market expectations.

1. Measuring Market Sentiment Through Fundamental Data

Fundamental analysis can reveal market sentiment by examining broader economic and company-specific news that affects investor attitudes. For example:

- **Consumer Confidence Index (CCI)**: This index gauges consumer optimism or pessimism about the economy. A rising CCI suggests consumers feel secure in their economic prospects, which can drive up spending and, consequently, stock prices. For options traders, a high CCI may signal potential gains for retail and consumer-oriented stocks.

- **Corporate Announcements and Earnings Guidance**: When a company provides optimistic future earnings guidance, it may boost investor sentiment and drive up demand for call options on that company's stock. Conversely, a profit warning or negative earnings revision may spur bearish sentiment, which could increase the demand for put options.

2. Sentiment-Based Options Strategies

Several options strategies can help traders leverage changes in market sentiment:

a. Long Straddle and Long Strangle

These strategies, discussed earlier in relation to earnings reports, can also apply to shifts in market sentiment. When sentiment is expected to cause significant price movements, traders may use a straddle or strangle to capitalize on that volatility.

b. Bull and Bear Call Spreads

Bull call spreads involve buying a call option at a lower strike price and selling another call at a higher strike price. This strategy is profitable if the asset price rises moderately, aligning with a bullish sentiment. Conversely, a bear call spread is suitable for bearish sentiment, where the trader expects the asset price to fall or remain stagnant.

c. Calendar Spreads

Calendar spreads, where options with the same strike price but different expiration dates are traded, can help traders profit from expected sentiment shifts. For example, if bullish sentiment is expected to strengthen gradually, a trader might purchase a longer-term call and sell a near-term call at the same strike price. This structure allows the trader to benefit from short-term time decay while positioning for a future price rise.

Sector and Industry Analysis for Informed Options Trading

In addition to individual company performance, sector and industry trends can influence options trades. Understanding these trends helps traders determine which industries are likely to outperform or underperform based on economic and market cycles.

1. Analyzing Sector Performance

Different sectors react uniquely to economic events, making them suitable for specific options trades during different phases of the economic cycle. For example:

- **Defensive Sectors**: These sectors, which include utilities, healthcare, and consumer staples, tend to perform well in economic downturns. During times of market instability, options traders might consider call options on defensive stocks, as they are less likely to experience large declines in value.
- **Cyclical Sectors**: Cyclical sectors, such as technology, financials, and consumer discretionary, are sensitive to economic expansions and contractions. During periods of economic growth, call options on stocks within these sectors may be advantageous, while during contractions, traders might prefer protective puts or bear call spreads.

2. Sector-Specific Strategies

Several options strategies are well-suited for sector-based trading:

a. Sector Rotation

Sector rotation is a strategy that capitalizes on the natural ebb and flow of different sectors during various economic phases. For example, as the economy shifts from expansion to recession, options traders might move from technology and industrial sectors to healthcare or consumer staples.

b. Pairs Trading with Options

Pairs trading involves taking opposing positions in two correlated assets, such as two companies in the same sector. In options, this could mean buying a call on one stock while purchasing a put on another, effectively betting on the performance disparity within the sector. For instance, if two companies in the technology sector have diverging earnings prospects, a pairs trade might involve calls on the more promising stock and puts on the weaker one.

Combining Fundamental and Technical Analysis for Options Trading

While fundamental analysis offers insight into a company's intrinsic value and overall market conditions, technical analysis can provide a shorter-term view of price patterns and momentum. Integrating both types of analysis allows options traders to make well-rounded decisions by aligning long-term value with short-term timing.

1. Identifying Key Entry and Exit Points

One challenge of fundamental analysis in options trading is the difficulty in pinpointing precise entry and exit points. By incorporating technical analysis indicators, traders can improve timing. Some commonly used technical tools in conjunction with fundamental analysis include:

- **Moving Averages**: Moving averages, such as the 50-day or 200-day averages, help identify trends. If a stock fundamentally appears strong but recently broke above its 200-day moving average, this bullish signal can reinforce a call option strategy.
- **Relative Strength Index (RSI)**: RSI measures overbought and oversold conditions. If the RSI indicates an oversold position while fundamentals suggest long-term growth, it may signal an attractive entry point for buying calls.

2. The Role of Volatility Indicators

Since options are heavily influenced by volatility, indicators like the CBOE Volatility Index (VIX) and implied volatility are crucial. Options traders can use the VIX to gauge market-wide volatility trends. A high VIX might suggest it's time to consider volatility-based strategies, such as straddles or strangles, especially if there is a fundamental reason for expected price swings.

Risk Management and Fundamental Analysis in Options Trading

Managing risk is a cornerstone of successful options trading, especially when relying on fundamental analysis. Since markets can behave unpredictably, prudent risk management protects against unforeseen losses.

1. Setting Position Size and Exposure Limits

Traders should define clear rules for how much of their capital they are willing to allocate to a single trade, sector, or company. A trader might cap their position size at 2% to 5% of their portfolio, limiting potential losses from any single trade.

2. Using Stop Loss Orders and Protective Puts

Stop-loss orders automatically close a position if it reaches a predetermined price, reducing the risk of further losses. For example, if a trader purchases a call option on a company expected to report strong earnings but wants to limit exposure, they might set a stop-loss at a specific point.

Protective puts are another effective strategy. By purchasing a put on a stock they own, traders can hedge against downside risk. This strategy is particularly useful if the fundamental analysis is sound, but there's potential for short-term volatility.

3. Diversification Across Sectors and Strategies

Diversifying across sectors, industries, and strategies can reduce the impact of sector-specific or economic downturns. For example, a trader who has call options in the technology sector might balance this with puts in cyclical sectors like consumer discretionary, which tend to underperform in an economic slowdown.

Evaluating Long-Term Market and Industry Trends

Long-term macroeconomic and industry trends can help traders position for enduring shifts that may affect the value of options over extended periods. These trends are often less volatile than quarterly earnings or sentiment shifts, providing stable opportunities for options traders who can identify them early.

1. Technology and Innovation Trends

Technological innovations, such as advancements in artificial intelligence, renewable energy, and healthcare, create new market opportunities. For example, options traders might focus on companies leading in electric vehicle production or renewable energy as these sectors are poised for long-term growth. Call options on leaders in innovative fields can provide exposure to these growth trends.

2. Regulatory and Policy Changes

Government policies, particularly in industries like finance, healthcare, and energy, can have lasting impacts on stock performance. Options traders can benefit by staying informed of regulatory trends, positioning themselves in options on companies likely to benefit from or be hindered by policy changes.

Fundamental analysis equips options traders with valuable insights into a company's financial health, sector performance, and broader economic trends. By understanding how to evaluate financial statements, interpret economic data, and anticipate market sentiment shifts, traders can make more informed options trades and potentially improve their outcomes.

Combining fundamental analysis with technical tools can refine timing, while diversification and risk management strategies protect against unexpected market movements. As markets evolve, traders who leverage fundamental insights — from earnings trends and economic data to sector shifts and long-term macro trends — position themselves to navigate the complexities of options trading with greater precision and confidence.

Chapter 11

Technical Analysis and Charting Basics

In options trading, understanding the market goes beyond just monitoring price trends. Technical analysis provides a framework for analyzing historical price movements, identifying patterns, and using these insights to predict future market behavior. This chapter will cover essential technical analysis tools, popular chart patterns, and key indicators that traders use to gain an edge in options trading. By mastering these elements, traders can make more informed decisions on entry and exit points, increasing their likelihood of profitable trades.

Introduction to Technical Analysis

Technical analysis, unlike fundamental analysis, focuses on analyzing past price movements and volume to predict future trends. In the context of options trading, understanding technical patterns can provide traders with a sharper view of potential price changes. By recognizing these patterns, traders can anticipate volatility, momentum, and potential reversals, all of which can heavily impact options prices and trading decisions.

Technical analysis is rooted in three main principles:

- **Prices move in trends**: Recognizing that prices follow patterns rather than moving randomly is essential for predicting future movements.
- **Price history tends to repeat**: Human behavior and market psychology cause certain patterns to reoccur, providing a basis for technical predictions.
- **Market action reflects all known information**: Technical analysts believe that the current price reflects all information, making it a self-contained indicator for future behavior.

These principles form the foundation of technical analysis, setting the stage for understanding various chart patterns and indicators.

Understanding Stock Charts

Charts are the backbone of technical analysis. They represent historical price movements in visual formats, helping traders interpret trends, volatility, and trading volume.

a) Types of Stock Charts

There are several types of charts that traders use, but the three most popular in technical analysis are line charts, bar charts, and candlestick charts.

- **Line Chart**: This type connects the closing prices over a set period with a continuous line. While simple, it's often used to observe trends over time.
- **Bar Chart**: Bar charts display the open, high, low, and close (OHLC) prices within a given period. This chart is useful for observing volatility and pinpointing price fluctuations within a trading session.
- **Candlestick Chart**: A favorite among technical analysts, candlestick charts also display OHLC information but with a more visual representation. The body of each "candlestick" shows the range between the open and close prices, and the wicks (or shadows) show the high and low. Candlesticks are particularly helpful for identifying trends and patterns in trading sessions.

Candlestick patterns, in particular, can provide insights into market sentiment, identifying where buyers and sellers are exerting influence.

Popular Chart Patterns

Chart patterns are formations created by price movements on a chart, reflecting shifts in market sentiment. Recognizing these patterns helps traders make educated assumptions about future price movements, providing potential entry and exit points.

a) Head and Shoulders

The head and shoulders pattern is a reversal pattern that signals a change from bullish to bearish or vice versa. It consists of three peaks: the central peak (the head) is higher than the two outside peaks (the shoulders). When this pattern appears after an uptrend, it suggests the price may begin to decline, marking an ideal moment for options traders to consider bearish positions.

b) Double Top and Double Bottom

The double top pattern forms after a price reaches a peak, pulls back, and then attempts to rise to the same level again. This pattern signifies that buyers failed to push the price higher, and a bearish trend may follow. Conversely, a double bottom occurs when the price hits a low, rebounds, and retests that low again, suggesting a bullish reversal may be near.

c) Cup and Handle

The cup and handle is a bullish continuation pattern. It appears when the price creates a rounded bottom (cup), followed by a smaller pullback (handle). The pattern signals that buyers are consolidating before pushing the price higher. Options traders may use this pattern to identify potential breakout opportunities.

d) Flags and Pennants

Flags and pennants are continuation patterns that indicate a pause in the prevailing trend. These patterns form after a sharp price movement, often accompanied by high volume. In a bullish flag, the price consolidates in a downward-sloping channel, while in a bearish flag, it consolidates upward. Pennants are similar but take the shape of a small symmetrical triangle. Both patterns suggest that a strong move in the direction of the prevailing trend may follow the consolidation.

Key Technical Indicators for Options Traders

Technical indicators are mathematical calculations based on price, volume, or open interest. They're used alongside chart patterns to provide insights into market conditions, helping options traders to time their positions.

a) Moving Averages

Moving averages smooth out price data to identify trends by creating a constantly updated average price. The two most commonly used types are the simple moving average (SMA) and the exponential moving average (EMA).

- **SMA** averages closing prices over a specified period, such as 50 or 200 days, providing a straightforward trend analysis.
- **EMA**, by contrast, gives more weight to recent prices, making it more responsive to recent price changes.

Moving averages can also be used to identify support and resistance levels. When the price crosses above the moving average, it's often seen as a bullish signal; conversely, a price crossing below may indicate a bearish signal.

b) Relative Strength Index (RSI)

The RSI is a momentum oscillator that measures the speed and change of price movements on a scale of 0 to 100. Readings above 70 suggest overbought conditions, while readings below 30 indicate oversold conditions.

RSI helps options traders gauge the strength of a trend, making it useful for identifying potential reversals.

c) Moving Average Convergence Divergence (MACD)

The MACD is a trend-following indicator that shows the relationship between two moving averages—typically the 12-day EMA and the 26-day EMA. It's composed of three parts: the MACD line, the signal line, and the histogram. When the MACD crosses above the signal line, it's considered a bullish signal, whereas a cross below is bearish.

d) Bollinger Bands

Bollinger Bands consist of a middle band (usually a 20-day SMA) and two outer bands placed two standard deviations above and below the middle band. These bands expand and contract with volatility, providing a measure of market volatility. When the price moves close to the outer bands, it suggests that the asset is overbought or oversold, indicating potential reversal points.

Using Technical Analysis for Options Trading

When applied to options, technical analysis helps traders make more calculated decisions on strike prices and expiration dates. For instance, using technical indicators to determine support and resistance levels can help set strike prices for call and put options in a way that maximizes potential profit while controlling risk.

Combining Technical Indicators with Options Strategies

One effective approach for options traders is to combine indicators like RSI and MACD to confirm signals. For instance, a trader might look for an overbought reading on the RSI alongside a bearish MACD crossover to support the decision to purchase put options.

Combining technical indicators allows options traders to refine their strategies, enhancing the reliability of their predictions. By layering multiple indicators, traders can reduce the chances of false signals and improve timing. Here are some examples of how combinations of indicators can create powerful options trading strategies:

a) RSI and MACD for Confirmation

When using the Relative Strength Index (RSI) alongside the Moving Average Convergence Divergence (MACD), traders seek alignment between overbought or oversold conditions (RSI) and momentum changes (MACD). For example, if the RSI indicates an overbought condition (above 70), and the MACD crosses below its signal line, this can suggest that momentum is shifting downward. This dual confirmation might encourage a trader to consider a bearish options strategy, such as buying put options or creating a bear put spread.

b) Moving Averages and Bollinger Bands for Trend Analysis

Moving averages can be combined with Bollinger Bands to identify potential breakout points in a trend. For instance, if the price breaks above the upper Bollinger Band while crossing above the 50-day moving average, it may signal a strong upward momentum, suggesting a potential entry point for call options. Conversely, if the price moves below the lower Bollinger Band and the moving average, it could indicate a bearish trend, supporting a put options strategy.

c) Using Multiple Timeframes for a Clearer Perspective

Analyzing technical indicators across different timeframes provides a broader context for trading decisions. For instance, a trader might use a long-term chart to identify the primary trend and a shorter-term chart for entry and exit points. If the 200-day moving average on the daily chart shows a strong upward trend, while the shorter 20-day moving average on an hourly chart crosses upward, it may signal a good moment to enter a call option trade that aligns with the overall trend. This multi-timeframe analysis can be particularly effective in options trading, where timing is crucial due to the impact of time decay on options value.

Practical Applications of Technical Analysis in Options Trading

Applying technical analysis to options trading involves not only identifying patterns and trends but also understanding how these insights translate into actionable strategies. Here are some practical examples:

a) Using Technical Analysis for Short-Term Options Trades

For short-term options trades, such as weekly options, technical analysis becomes especially valuable. Weekly options are highly sensitive to price movements because of their limited time frame, so traders often use shorter-term indicators, like the 5-day or 10-day moving averages, to capture rapid shifts. Chart patterns like flags, pennants, and triangle formations can provide quick insights into price consolidations and potential breakouts, helping traders decide when to enter or exit a position.

b) Applying Technical Analysis to Volatility Strategies

Volatility-based strategies, such as straddles and strangles, benefit from indicators that track price swings and volatility levels. Bollinger Bands, for example, help traders assess whether an asset is in a period of high or low volatility. If Bollinger Bands are wide apart, it suggests high volatility, which could make a straddle strategy more effective since larger price swings would be expected. Conversely, if the bands are narrow, it may signal low volatility, favoring strategies like an iron condor that profit from stable price movements.

c) Trend Following with Moving Averages in Options

Traders who use trend-following strategies in options trading can leverage moving averages to define the trend direction and strength. By using moving average crossovers, such as when the 50-day moving average crosses above the 200-day moving average (known as a "golden cross"), traders can confirm a bullish trend and consider call options or bullish spreads. In contrast, if the 50-day moving average crosses below the 200-day moving average (a "death cross"), it can signal a bearish trend, encouraging traders to explore put options or bearish spread strategies.

Risk Management in Technical Analysis-Based Options Trading

While technical analysis provides valuable insights, it's crucial to remember that no strategy is infallible. Options traders should implement risk management measures to protect against potential losses.

a) Setting Stop Losses

Stop losses are essential in options trading, especially when using technical analysis to time trades. For example, if a trader enters a call option trade based on a moving average crossover but the price starts moving against the trend, a stop loss can limit the potential loss. Placing a stop loss below a recent support level, identified through technical analysis, helps ensure that losses are manageable if the trend reverses.

b) Position Sizing and Diversification

Proper position sizing is another critical element of risk management in options trading. Even if technical indicators strongly suggest a certain price movement, it's wise to avoid over-committing to a single trade. By keeping individual trade sizes within a set percentage of the total portfolio, traders can spread their risk across multiple positions, reducing the impact of any one loss.

c) Recognizing and Avoiding Overtrading

One common pitfall in technical analysis is overtrading. With so many indicators and chart patterns available, it's easy for traders to see patterns where none exist, leading to unnecessary trades. To avoid this, it's helpful to develop a specific trading plan that includes clear entry and exit criteria based on a few well-understood indicators, rather than constantly switching strategies or adding indicators.

Limitations of Technical Analysis in Options Trading

Although technical analysis is a powerful tool, it has limitations, especially in options trading. Understanding these limitations helps traders use technical analysis effectively and avoid common misconceptions.

a) False Signals and Market Noise

Technical indicators can sometimes produce false signals, especially during periods of low trading volume or high market volatility. A moving average crossover, for example, might appear to signal a trend change, only to quickly reverse in the face of sudden news or macroeconomic developments. Options traders should use additional confirmation methods, such as multiple indicators, to filter out false signals.

b) Time Decay in Options

Options are time-sensitive instruments, and technical analysis doesn't account for the time decay (theta) that impacts options prices as expiration approaches. Even if a technical pattern suggests a strong move in the underlying asset, if the option is close to expiration, the value may not increase as expected due to time decay. This makes it essential for options traders to consider expiration dates alongside technical signals when planning trades.

c) Impact of Major Market Events

Technical analysis relies on historical price data, which may not account for unprecedented events like economic crises, natural disasters, or major political shifts. These events can drastically alter market behavior and render technical patterns ineffective. In options trading, where timing is critical, external factors should be monitored in tandem with technical analysis, helping traders avoid making decisions based solely on historical price movements.

Chapter 12

Options Trading Psychology

Options trading is not just about strategies, market conditions, or technical analysis; it fundamentally hinges on psychology. The mental aspect of trading can dictate success or failure more than any specific strategy or market insight. Understanding how to manage emotions, maintain discipline, and cultivate a solid trading mindset is crucial for anyone looking to thrive in the volatile world of options trading. This chapter will explore these psychological components in depth, offering insights and strategies to enhance your trading performance.

Understanding Trading Psychology

Trading psychology refers to the emotional and mental state of a trader, which influences their decision-making and ultimately their performance in the market. The emotions associated with trading—fear, greed, hope, and regret—can lead to irrational behavior, affecting not just individual trades but overall trading success.

The Impact of Emotions on Trading Decisions

Emotions can cloud judgment, causing traders to make decisions based on feelings rather than rational analysis. Here's how common emotions affect trading:

1. **Fear**: This is perhaps the most significant emotion in trading. Fear can stem from the possibility of losing money, missing out on a profitable trade (FOMO), or the volatility of the market. Traders might become overly cautious, leading them to miss opportunities or exit positions prematurely.
2. **Greed**: Conversely, greed can compel traders to take excessive risks. This emotion often arises when traders have experienced recent successes. They may overestimate their capabilities and pursue high-risk trades, which can lead to substantial losses.
3. **Hope**: Traders often cling to the hope that a losing trade will turn around. This hope can result in holding onto losing positions longer than necessary, often leading to greater losses.
4. **Regret**: After a loss, regret can lead to revenge trading—attempting to make back lost money through impulsive decisions. This often results in further losses.

Understanding these emotional triggers is the first step toward mitigating their effects. By recognizing when emotions are influencing your decisions, you can take steps to counteract them.

Developing Emotional Awareness

Emotional awareness is the ability to recognize and understand your emotions as they arise. For traders, this means being able to identify how feelings influence decisions. Here are some strategies to develop emotional awareness:

1. Self-Reflection and Journaling

Keeping a trading journal is a powerful tool for self-reflection. Documenting your trades, including your thoughts and emotions during each trade, can help you identify patterns in your behavior. Over time, you can analyze your successes and failures, allowing you to recognize when emotions are driving your decisions.

2. Mindfulness Practices

Mindfulness involves being present in the moment and observing your thoughts and feelings without judgment. Techniques such as meditation or breathing exercises can help traders develop mindfulness, enabling them to remain calm and focused during market fluctuations. This practice can also assist in reducing impulsivity, helping traders make decisions based on logic rather than emotion.

3. Emotional Regulation Techniques

Learning to manage emotions through regulation techniques can enhance trading performance. Techniques might include:

- **Cognitive Behavioral Strategies**: These involve challenging negative thoughts and replacing them with more positive or realistic ones. For example, instead of thinking, "I will never recover from this loss," you might reframe it to, "This is a learning experience that will help me make better decisions in the future."
- **Positive Visualization**: Visualizing successful trades can help build confidence and reduce anxiety. Spend time imagining your successful trading scenarios to reinforce a positive mindset.

The Importance of Discipline in Trading

Discipline is the cornerstone of successful trading. It involves following a well-defined trading plan without deviating due to emotional impulses. Here are key aspects of maintaining discipline:

1. Creating a Trading Plan

A solid trading plan outlines your strategies, risk management rules, and specific goals. This plan should include:

- **Entry and Exit Criteria**: Define when you will enter and exit trades based on your analysis.
- **Risk Management Rules**: Set strict rules for how much of your capital you are willing to risk on each trade. A common rule is to risk no more than 1-2% of your total trading capital on a single trade.
- **Performance Metrics**: Establish how you will evaluate your trades and adjust your strategies accordingly.

Once your trading plan is in place, sticking to it is critical. During times of emotional turmoil or market volatility, a well-defined plan will act as your guide, helping you resist the temptation to make impulsive decisions.

2. Setting Realistic Goals

Setting achievable trading goals can help maintain discipline. Goals should be specific, measurable, attainable, relevant, and time-bound (SMART). For instance, instead of saying, "I want to be a successful trader," you might set a goal like, "I aim to achieve a 10% return on my capital over the next six months."

3. Avoiding Overtrading

Overtrading occurs when a trader takes too many positions in an attempt to recover losses or chase after profits. This behavior can lead to emotional exhaustion and poor decision-making. To combat this, stick to your trading plan and avoid impulsively entering trades outside your defined strategy.

Cultivating a Winning Mindset

Beyond emotional management and discipline, cultivating a winning mindset is essential for long-term success in options trading. This mindset involves several components:

1. Embracing a Growth Mindset

A growth mindset is the belief that your skills and abilities can improve with effort and experience. In trading, this means viewing losses as opportunities for learning rather than as failures. Embracing a growth mindset allows you to adapt, learn from mistakes, and continuously improve your strategies.

2. Developing Resilience

Resilience is the ability to bounce back from setbacks. In trading, losses are inevitable, and how you respond to them can greatly affect your future success. Developing resilience involves:

- **Accepting Losses**: Understand that every trader experiences losses. Accepting this reality can help you detach emotionally from trades.
- **Staying Focused on the Long Term**: Rather than getting caught up in individual trades, focus on your long-term performance. This perspective can help reduce emotional reactions to short-term fluctuations.

3. Continuous Learning

The markets are constantly evolving, and successful traders commit to lifelong learning. Engage with educational resources, attend trading seminars, and connect with other traders to share insights and strategies. This commitment to learning not only improves your skills but also enhances your confidence as you become more knowledgeable.

The Role of Risk Management in Trading Psychology

Effective risk management is integral to options trading and significantly impacts a trader's psychological state. Understanding and managing risk can reduce anxiety and foster a more confident trading approach. Here are critical components of risk management relevant to trading psychology:

1. Defining Your Risk Tolerance

Risk tolerance is the degree of variability in investment returns that an investor is willing to withstand. This personal assessment should reflect your financial situation, trading experience, and emotional capacity to handle losses. By defining your risk tolerance, you can make informed decisions that align with your psychological comfort level.

2. Utilizing Stop-Loss Orders

Stop-loss orders are a critical tool for risk management. By setting predetermined exit points for trades, you can limit potential losses and reduce the emotional strain of decision-making during volatile market conditions. Knowing that you have a plan in place can enhance your confidence and allow for a more focused approach.

3. Diversifying Your Portfolio

Diversification involves spreading investments across various assets to reduce risk. A well-diversified portfolio can help mitigate the psychological impact of significant losses in any single position, as the overall portfolio value is less likely to be affected dramatically. This strategy can provide peace of mind and reduce anxiety associated with market fluctuations.

The Importance of Community and Support

Having a support network can play a vital role in your psychological well-being as a trader. Engaging with a community of traders can provide emotional support, reduce feelings of isolation, and foster a culture of shared learning. Here are some ways to build a supportive trading community:

1. Joining Trading Groups

Participating in online forums, social media groups, or local trading clubs can help you connect with other traders. Sharing experiences, strategies, and challenges can provide valuable insights and reassurance that you are not alone in your trading journey.

2. Finding a Mentor

Working with a mentor who has more experience in options trading can provide guidance and help you navigate the psychological challenges of trading. A mentor can offer insights into managing emotions, maintaining discipline, and developing a successful trading mindset.

3. Accountability Partners

Having a trading buddy can create a system of accountability. Regular check-ins with a partner can help you stay disciplined, discuss strategies, and share your emotional experiences, which can lighten the psychological burden of trading.

Trading psychology plays a critical role in the success of options traders. By understanding and managing emotions, maintaining discipline, and cultivating a resilient mindset, traders can improve their decision-making processes and overall performance. Options trading is inherently challenging, but by prioritizing psychological readiness alongside technical skills, you can navigate the complexities of the market more effectively.

As you continue your trading journey, remember that mastering the psychological aspect of trading is an ongoing process. Be patient with yourself, and recognize that growth comes from both success and failure. By committing to self-improvement and adopting a proactive approach to trading psychology, you will position yourself for greater success in the world of options trading.

Chapter 13

Building a Personalized Options Trading Plan

Creating a personalized options trading plan is a critical step for traders seeking to navigate the complexities of the options market successfully. A well-structured plan not only establishes clear goals but also defines strategies and sets risk limits tailored to individual trading styles and risk tolerances. In this chapter, we will guide you through the essential components of developing a personalized options trading plan, ensuring that it is realistic, comprehensive, and adaptable to changing market conditions.

A robust trading plan functions as a trader's roadmap, guiding decision-making and ensuring that strategies align with personal and financial goals. This chapter will emphasize the significance of each component of a trading plan, the psychology of trading, and practical steps to formulate a plan that suits your unique trading approach.

Understanding the Importance of a Trading Plan

Why a Trading Plan Matters

A trading plan serves as a roadmap for your trading journey. It provides direction and discipline, which are vital in a market often characterized by volatility and unpredictability. Without a plan, traders may fall into impulsive decision-making based on emotions or market hype, leading to inconsistent results and potential losses.

Consider this: a study conducted by the American Psychological Association indicates that traders who adhere to a well-defined plan are more likely to make informed decisions rather than succumb to emotional impulses, thereby improving their trading performance (Baker & Ricciardi, 2014). Additionally, a trading plan helps in quantifying performance, allowing for a structured approach to review and adjustment, which is crucial in refining one's strategies over time.

Components of a Successful Trading Plan

A successful trading plan typically includes:

1. **Goals**: Clear and measurable objectives that define what you want to achieve through options trading.
2. **Strategies**: Specific methods and approaches you will use to enter and exit trades.
3. **Risk Management**: Guidelines on how to manage risk, including position sizing and stop-loss orders.
4. **Review Process**: A system for evaluating your trades and making adjustments as necessary.

Each of these components plays a crucial role in ensuring that the trading plan is not only effective but also sustainable over the long term.

Setting Goals for Your Trading Plan

Defining Your Objectives

The first step in building a personalized options trading plan is to set clear goals. Consider both short-term and long-term objectives. Short-term goals may include monthly profit targets or improving your trading skills, while long-term goals could focus on achieving a certain percentage return on investment over several years.

SMART Goals Framework

To ensure that your goals are effective, use the SMART criteria, which stand for:

- **Specific**: Clearly define what you want to achieve. Instead of saying, "I want to make money," specify how much and by when.
- **Measurable**: Quantify your goals so you can track progress. For example, "I want to achieve a 10% return on my capital within the next quarter."
- **Achievable**: Set realistic goals that challenge you but are attainable. Consider your trading experience and market conditions.
- **Relevant**: Ensure your goals align with your overall trading strategy and personal circumstances. Goals should reflect what is important to you in your trading journey.
- **Time-bound**: Assign a deadline to create a sense of urgency. For instance, "I will complete my training on options strategies within the next month."

Examples of Trading Goals

- **Short-term Goal**: Achieve a monthly return of 5% on your trading capital over the next three months, using a specified strategy.

- **Long-term Goal**: Build a trading portfolio that averages a 15% annual return over the next five years by diversifying across multiple strategies and assets.

These goals should be written down and revisited regularly to assess progress and make necessary adjustments.

Developing Your Trading Strategy

Identifying Your Trading Style

Your trading strategy should align with your individual trading style, risk tolerance, and market outlook. Consider whether you prefer short-term trading, such as day trading or swing trading, or longer-term strategies, such as buy-and-hold.

- **Day Trading**: Involves executing multiple trades within a single day, capitalizing on small price movements. This approach requires a solid understanding of market dynamics and technical analysis.
- **Swing Trading**: Focuses on capturing price movements over several days to weeks. Traders typically use technical analysis to identify entry and exit points.

- **Long-Term Trading**: This style involves holding positions for an extended period, often based on fundamental analysis. Options strategies like covered calls or protective puts can complement this approach.

Popular Options Trading Strategies

Here are some common strategies to consider when developing your trading plan:

1. **Covered Call**: Involves holding a long position in an asset and selling call options on that same asset to generate income. This strategy can enhance returns in a flat or moderately bullish market.
2. **Protective Put**: Purchasing a put option to protect against a decline in the value of an asset you own. This acts as insurance and can help limit losses.
3. **Straddle**: Buying both a call and a put option at the same strike price, anticipating significant movement in either direction. This strategy benefits from volatility, regardless of the direction.
4. **Strangle**: Similar to a straddle but involves buying call and put options at different strike prices. This can be a cost-effective way to capitalize on expected volatility.

5. **Iron Condor**: A strategy that involves selling an out-of-the-money call and put option while simultaneously buying a further out-of-the-money call and put option. This strategy is designed to profit from low volatility and ranges in the underlying asset.

Tailoring Strategies to Your Goals

Select strategies that align with your trading goals. For instance, if your goal is to generate consistent income, covered calls might be a suitable choice. Conversely, if you aim to capitalize on volatility, straddles or strangles could be more appropriate.

Furthermore, it's crucial to backtest your strategies using historical data. This helps you understand how a particular strategy might have performed in various market conditions, providing insights into potential risks and rewards.

Risk Management in Options Trading

Understanding Risk Tolerance

Risk tolerance varies from trader to trader. Assess your financial situation, investment experience, and emotional resilience to determine how much risk you can comfortably take. This assessment will help you set appropriate risk limits in your trading plan.

It's important to recognize that trading inherently involves risk, and psychological factors such as fear and greed can significantly influence your decisions. Understanding your emotional triggers can aid in developing a plan that keeps you grounded.

Position Sizing

Position sizing is a crucial aspect of risk management. Determine how much capital you will allocate to each trade based on your overall portfolio size and risk tolerance. A common rule is to risk no more than 1-2% of your trading capital on a single trade.

For example, if your trading account has $10,000, you should consider risking no more than $100 to $200 on any one trade. This approach helps mitigate potential losses and allows you to withstand a series of losing trades without significantly impacting your overall capital.

Stop-Loss Orders

Incorporating stop-loss orders into your trading plan can help limit losses. A stop-loss order automatically sells your option position when it reaches a predetermined price, helping to mitigate potential losses if the market moves against you.

Setting stop-loss levels should be based on technical analysis or a fixed percentage of the position size. For instance, if you set a stop-loss at 10% below your entry price, your risk is predefined, allowing you to manage your exposure effectively.

Diversification

Diversifying your options positions across different assets or strategies can also help manage risk. By spreading your investments, you reduce the impact of any single trade on your overall portfolio.

Consider diversifying across various sectors or asset classes, such as stocks, ETFs, or commodities. This approach not only helps mitigate risk but can also enhance your potential for returns, as different markets may respond differently to economic events.

Creating a Review and Adjustment Process

Regularly Reviewing Your Trading Plan

Establish a routine for reviewing your trading performance. Analyze your trades to identify patterns, strengths, and areas for improvement. This review process allows you to refine your strategies and enhance your decision-making.

Consider maintaining a trading journal where you document each trade, including your rationale for entering or exiting positions, emotions experienced, and lessons learned. This practice helps you to gain insights over time and recognize patterns in your behavior that may impact your trading results.

Adapting to Market Conditions

The options market is dynamic, and conditions can change rapidly. Your trading plan should be flexible enough to adapt to new information, shifts in market sentiment, or changes in your financial situation. Regularly reassess your goals, strategies, and risk limits to ensure they remain relevant.

For instance, if market volatility increases significantly, you may need to adjust your strategies or increase your risk management measures. Staying informed about macroeconomic trends and market news can provide valuable context for these adjustments.

Building a personalized options trading plan is essential for successful trading. By setting clear goals, developing tailored strategies, managing risk, and establishing a review process, you position yourself for long-term success in the options market. Remember that trading is a journey, and continuous learning and adaptation are key components of that journey.

Your trading plan should be a living document that evolves as you gain more experience and as market conditions change. The discipline to follow your plan, combined with the flexibility to adapt it when necessary, can set you on the path to achieving your trading objectives.

Chapter 14

Review of Key Strategies

In this final chapter, we'll revisit the core strategies for beginners in options trading, highlighting the importance of consistency, patience, and continued learning. For newcomers, it's easy to get caught up in the excitement of options trading without fully understanding the principles needed for long-term success. This chapter serves as a strategic roadmap to reinforce the foundations you've built throughout the book and provide guidance on how to deepen your knowledge over time.

Options trading is an ever-evolving discipline; strategies that work in one market cycle may require adjustments in another. To continue growing as a trader, staying adaptable, practicing patience, and accessing credible resources are essential. Let's start by summarizing the main strategies discussed, then examine ways to further develop your trading skills, and finally, explore additional resources to keep you informed and competent in this field.

Summary of Main Strategies for Beginners

1. Covered Calls

A covered call strategy is one of the safest approaches for beginners and involves selling call options on assets you already own. This allows you to earn premium income while holding a long position in the stock. It's a lower-risk strategy ideal for investors who wish to generate passive income with moderate exposure to options.

Key Benefits

- **Income Generation**: Selling calls provides a premium, adding regular income from stock positions.
- **Limited Downside Risk**: The risk is limited to the stock's price decline since the trader already owns the stock.

Important Considerations

- **Capped Upside**: Profits are limited to the strike price of the sold call plus the premium, which means potential gains on the stock are restricted.

- **Requires Stock Ownership**: This strategy requires holding the stock, making it capital-intensive.

Covered calls are particularly well-suited to conservative investors looking to boost returns on stocks they already hold, especially when they anticipate little movement in the stock's price.

2. Protective Puts

Protective puts act as an insurance policy on stocks you own. By buying a put option, you can secure a minimum sale price, thereby limiting potential losses if the stock price falls.

Key Benefits

- **Risk Management**: Protective puts provide downside protection, especially in volatile markets.
- **Flexibility**: Traders can set a "floor" for losses without selling the stock, maintaining the potential for upward gains.

Important Considerations

- **Cost of the Premium**: Buying a put option incurs a premium cost, which could reduce net gains if the stock doesn't fall.

- **Strike Price Selection**: Choosing the right strike price is crucial; higher strike prices increase the premium but provide more protection.

This strategy is valuable for those holding volatile stocks and looking to avoid significant losses without divesting their positions. It's especially useful during periods of economic uncertainty.

3. Long Call and Long Put Options

Long calls and long puts allow beginners to leverage options to gain significant exposure to stock price movements with limited upfront capital. A long call benefits from price increases, while a long put profits when prices decline.

Key Benefits

- **Leverage**: These positions require a fraction of the cost of stock ownership, potentially increasing returns.
- **Defined Risk**: The risk is limited to the premium paid for the option.

Important Considerations

- **Time Decay**: Options lose value over time, which can erode gains if the stock moves too slowly.

- **Market Timing**: Long options require accurate timing to capitalize on price movements effectively.

Long calls and puts are ideal for traders expecting short-term price shifts and willing to accept the risk of losing the premium. Mastery of timing and market analysis is critical for success with these strategies.

4. Cash-Secured Puts

Selling cash-secured puts allows traders to earn a premium by agreeing to buy stock at a set price if it falls below the strike price. This strategy is suitable for traders interested in buying stock at a discount.

Key Benefits

- **Income Generation**: Selling a put provides upfront premium income.
- **Potential Stock Ownership**: If the stock price drops below the strike price, you may acquire the stock at a favorable price.

Important Considerations

- **Capital Requirement**: Traders must hold enough cash to buy the stock if assigned, which may limit flexibility.

- **Market Risk**: There's a risk of buying the stock at a strike price if it continues to decline further.

Cash-secured puts are a good fit for investors looking to acquire shares of a company at a lower price or generate steady income from premium collection.

5. Spread Strategies (Bull Call Spread, Bear Put Spread)

Spread strategies reduce the cost of entry by combining two options contracts. A bull call spread profits from a moderate rise in stock price, while a bear put spread is advantageous during slight price declines.

Key Benefits

- **Cost Efficiency**: Spread strategies reduce the overall cost of an options trade.
- **Limited Risk and Reward**: Potential losses are capped, making it easier to control risk.

Important Considerations

- **Moderate Gains**: The maximum profit is limited by the spread width, capping upside potential.
- **Complexity**: These strategies involve multiple transactions, which may increase fees and complexity for beginners.

Spread strategies are beneficial for traders with a moderate outlook on market movement who want to minimize upfront costs.

How to Continue Growing as an Options Trader

Learning to trade options successfully requires both technical knowledge and practical experience. Here are steps to keep advancing your skills:

1. Practice and Reflect on Trades

Trading options successfully requires a practical understanding of risk, timing, and the psychology of market movements. Start small with paper trading or limited capital in a brokerage account specifically for practice.

- **Paper Trading**: Many platforms offer simulated accounts where you can trade options without real money. This allows you to test strategies without financial risk.
- **Journaling**: Keep a journal to record every trade, including reasons, outcomes, and lessons learned.

Over time, this practice will help you identify patterns in your trading behavior.

2. Enhance Analytical Skills

Successful options traders continuously refine their ability to analyze both technical and fundamental data.

- **Technical Analysis**: Gain proficiency in chart patterns, price trends, and technical indicators such as moving averages and relative strength index (RSI). These tools help in assessing price direction and momentum.
- **Fundamental Analysis**: Understand key financial metrics, such as earnings reports and economic indicators. Company news, market sentiment, and broader economic trends also influence options prices and should be part of your analysis.

3. Understand and Adapt to Market Cycles

Market conditions can vary significantly, from bullish to bearish trends and low to high volatility. Being adaptable is crucial.

- **Trend Identification**: Learn to recognize different market cycles and adjust your strategies accordingly. Bull markets may favor long calls,

while bear markets may be suitable for long puts or protective puts.
- **Volatility Analysis**: Volatility affects options pricing; strategies like the iron condor and butterfly spread can be beneficial in high-volatility environments.

4. Risk Management and Discipline

Maintaining a disciplined approach to risk is key to long-term success.

- **Position Sizing**: Always manage the size of each trade relative to your overall portfolio. Risking only a small portion of your capital per trade can prevent significant losses.
- **Stop Loss and Exit Points**: Plan your exit points before entering a trade. Establishing rules for when to cut losses or take profits helps avoid emotional decisions.

5. Stay Informed and Educate Yourself

Options trading is influenced by global events, policy changes, and economic conditions. Following market news and continuing education can keep your skills sharp.

- **Industry News**: Regularly read financial news, especially related to sectors where you hold options positions.
- **Advanced Learning**: Consider courses or certifications that focus on options trading, such as the Chartered Market Technician (CMT) designation or specialized options courses from reputable institutions.

Additional Resources for Continuous Learning

To stay updated and knowledgeable, accessing reliable resources is invaluable. Here are recommended resources for continued education and support:

1. Books and Educational Material

- *Options as a Strategic Investment* by Lawrence G. McMillan: A classic guide with in-depth coverage of options strategies.
- *The Options Playbook* by Brian Overby: An accessible guide that explains complex strategies in simple terms.

2. Online Courses and Certifications

- **Options Industry Council (OIC)**: Offers free courses, webinars, and resources for all levels of options traders.
- **Coursera and Udemy**: Provide introductory and advanced courses on options trading from reputable educators and institutions.

3. Trading Platforms and Tools

- **ThinkorSwim by TD Ameritrade**: A comprehensive platform with paper trading, extensive charting tools, and educational resources.
- **Interactive Brokers**: Known for low-cost trades and robust analytics.

4. Industry Websites and Forums

- **Seeking Alpha and MarketWatch**: For daily financial news and analysis, helpful for tracking market trends.
- **Reddit (r/options)**: A forum where traders discuss strategies, share experiences, and ask questions.

Chapter 15

Final Thoughts on Options Trading for Financial Growth

As we reach the end of this journey into options trading, it's time to reflect on the crucial elements that will guide you toward success. The world of options can be both thrilling and daunting, demanding dedication, discipline, and a willingness to stay informed and adaptable. This chapter is crafted to provide actionable insights on navigating the future of options trading, ensuring you remain well-prepared to harness opportunities for financial growth in 2025 and beyond.

With the financial landscape constantly evolving, options traders must focus on three main pillars to maintain a competitive edge: staying informed in a changing market, prioritizing disciplined practice, and establishing a long-term growth strategy. Let's examine each of these aspects to equip you with the mindset and skills necessary for continued success in your trading endeavors.

Staying Informed in a Changing Market

1. The Importance of Ongoing Market Analysis

The financial markets are subject to continuous change, driven by factors such as economic data, geopolitical events, and shifts in investor sentiment. Options traders, in particular, need to be vigilant, as changes in market conditions directly affect volatility, interest rates, and options pricing.

Key Aspects of Market Analysis

- **Economic Indicators**: Reports on inflation, unemployment, GDP growth, and consumer spending offer critical insights into economic health and potential market reactions. Monitoring these indicators enables you to anticipate broad market trends and adjust your options strategy accordingly.
- **Geopolitical Events**: Global events—such as international conflicts, trade agreements, or regulatory shifts—can cause sudden changes in market sentiment. Options traders should stay informed about these developments and assess how they may affect different sectors or specific stocks.

- **Sector-Specific Trends**: Different sectors react uniquely to economic changes. For instance, technology stocks may be highly sensitive to interest rate hikes, while commodities are influenced by inflation and global supply chains. By focusing on sector-specific trends, you can better identify opportunities and manage risk.

2. Utilizing Advanced Data Tools

Access to comprehensive data and analysis tools can transform how you approach options trading. Many platforms now offer real-time data, advanced analytics, and predictive modeling, allowing traders to make more informed decisions.

Recommended Tools and Resources

- **Real-Time Data Platforms**: Services like Bloomberg Terminal, Refinitiv, and TradingView provide data feeds and analytics that help traders track market movements and identify patterns in real-time.
- **Technical Analysis Tools**: Indicators such as moving averages, relative strength index (RSI), and Bollinger Bands are essential for understanding price trends and market momentum. These tools are integrated into most

major trading platforms, helping traders make data-driven decisions.
- **Sentiment Analysis**: Social media and news sentiment analysis tools can gauge public opinion on a particular stock or sector, helping you identify potential spikes in volatility. Companies like Benzinga and Market Chameleon offer sentiment analysis for options trading.

3. Following Regulatory Changes

The financial industry is heavily regulated, and changes in regulatory policies can have substantial impacts on trading activities. Staying up-to-date on new policies ensures that you remain compliant and protects you from unexpected risks.

Key Regulatory Considerations

- **Tax Implications**: Options trading can have unique tax implications, especially in the U.S., where different tax treatments apply to short-term vs. long-term gains. Familiarizing yourself with the tax code, or consulting a tax professional, can help optimize your tax strategies.
- **Brokerage Requirements**: Brokers may adjust their margin and collateral requirements in response to regulatory shifts. Understanding these requirements allows you to avoid account

issues and ensure that your positions remain viable during times of increased market scrutiny.

Being proactive in monitoring regulatory developments can save you from costly errors and support a more sustainable trading strategy.

The Role of Practice and Discipline

1. Building a Consistent Trading Routine

Success in options trading requires more than understanding strategies—it involves developing a disciplined, consistent approach to executing and managing trades. A well-defined routine helps reinforce your knowledge, minimize emotional decision-making, and improve long-term profitability.

Key Components of a Trading Routine

- **Daily Market Review**: Begin each trading day by reviewing pre-market data, economic indicators, and news that could influence your positions. A thorough morning review primes you for the trading day and allows you to anticipate potential market movements.

- **Trade Journaling**: Maintaining a trading journal is invaluable for tracking performance and identifying areas for improvement. Include details on trade rationale, entry and exit points, and post-trade analysis to gain insights into your habits and biases.
- **End-of-Day Evaluation**: Reflecting on each day's trades can help you understand what went well and what didn't. Over time, this process will aid in developing a disciplined, consistent approach to risk management and strategy refinement.

2. Developing Emotional Resilience

One of the biggest challenges in options trading is managing emotions—particularly fear and greed. These emotions can drive impulsive actions, leading to suboptimal decisions and potential losses. Developing emotional resilience allows traders to stick to their strategies, even under stress.

Techniques for Building Emotional Discipline

- **Set Clear Rules**: Create predefined rules for entry and exit points, risk tolerance, and position sizing. Following these rules strictly minimizes the influence of emotions on your trades.

- **Meditation and Mindfulness**: Practicing mindfulness and meditation can help calm your mind and prevent rash decisions. Many successful traders use these techniques to stay focused and grounded during volatile market periods.
- **Accepting Losses as Part of the Process**: Losses are inevitable in options trading. Viewing them as learning opportunities rather than setbacks helps maintain a constructive mindset.

3. The Value of Backtesting and Paper Trading

Paper trading—practicing trades without real money—and backtesting—using historical data to test strategies—are essential components of a disciplined trading routine. They provide risk-free environments to experiment with new strategies, refine techniques, and build confidence.

Key Benefits of Paper Trading and Backtesting

- **Risk-Free Experimentation**: Both methods allow you to test strategies without exposing capital to actual market risk, making them ideal for beginners and experienced traders alike.
- **Gaining Practical Experience**: Paper trading simulates real trading conditions, helping you understand how strategies perform in different

market scenarios. This experience builds confidence and reduces hesitation when executing trades in live markets.
- **Identifying Weaknesses**: Backtesting strategies against historical data reveals weaknesses and areas for improvement. This insight is invaluable for developing and refining trading approaches.

Combining routine practice, emotional discipline, and practical testing of strategies lays a solid foundation for consistent, profitable trading.

Setting Yourself Up for Success in 2025 and Beyond

1. Developing a Long-Term Mindset

While options trading often focuses on short-term opportunities, a long-term perspective is essential for sustained success. By prioritizing gradual skill development, prudent risk management, and consistent profitability over rapid gains, you can build a more resilient trading career.

Benefits of a Long-Term Perspective

- **Reduced Stress and Pressure**: Viewing options trading as a long-term endeavor alleviates the pressure to constantly achieve short-term wins, making it easier to follow a disciplined strategy.
- **Continuous Learning**: Adopting a growth mindset encourages you to stay curious and committed to learning new strategies, tools, and techniques.
- **Portfolio Resilience**: Building a diversified, balanced portfolio over time helps cushion against market volatility, reducing the impact of individual losses.

2. Expanding Your Network and Seeking Mentorship

Learning from others—whether through online communities, mentorship, or professional groups—offers valuable insights and helps you avoid common pitfalls. Networking with experienced traders allows you to exchange strategies, gain constructive feedback, and stay motivated.

Ways to Connect with Experienced Traders

- **Trading Communities and Forums**: Platforms like Reddit (r/options), Elite Trader, and Trade2Win foster discussion and information exchange among traders. Participating in these

communities provides access to diverse perspectives and firsthand advice.
- **Professional Associations**: Organizations such as the Market Technicians Association (MTA) or Chartered Market Technician (CMT) programs offer resources, certifications, and networking opportunities for serious traders.
- **Mentorship Programs**: Many brokerage firms and financial institutions offer mentorship programs that pair beginners with experienced traders, providing one-on-one guidance and practical training.

Establishing a support network strengthens your trading skills, promotes accountability, and enhances your overall growth as a trader.

3. Setting Personal Goals and Benchmarks

Goal-setting is a powerful tool for ensuring progress in your trading journey. Establishing both short-term and long-term objectives helps you maintain motivation and track your improvement over time.

Steps for Effective Goal-Setting

- **Define Clear, Attainable Goals**: Break down broad objectives (e.g., increasing portfolio returns by 20%) into specific, measurable steps (e.g.,

improving trade selection, learning a new strategy).
- **Set Timeframes**: Assign timeframes to each goal to maintain accountability. Revisit these regularly to assess progress and make adjustments if necessary.
- **Reflect on Achievements**: Regularly celebrate your accomplishments, no matter how small. Recognizing progress reinforces positive behaviors and sustains motivation.

Tracking personal benchmarks provides clarity on where you are in your journey, offering valuable insights into areas of strength and opportunities for improvement.

4. Leveraging Technology for Efficiency and Insights

The role of technology in options trading cannot be overstated. With advancements in artificial intelligence, algorithmic trading, and real-time analytics, traders have access to tools that can vastly improve efficiency and precision.

Popular Technological Tools for Options Traders

- **Automated Trading Systems**: Many platforms now allow traders to set predefined rules for executing trades, reducing the need for constant monitoring and enhancing efficiency.

- **AI and Machine Learning Models**: Machine learning algorithms analyze vast amounts of data to identify patterns and predict future trends. While these models are complex, they can provide significant insights when integrated into trading strategies.
- **Mobile Trading Apps**: Many brokers offer mobile apps with real-time data, notifications, and order management, allowing traders to manage their portfolios on the go.

Integrating these technologies into your routine streamlines operations, reduces the potential for error, and provides a competitive edge in the fast-paced world of options trading.

As you conclude this journey, it's clear that options trading is a multifaceted, dynamic field requiring a blend of knowledge, discipline, and adaptability. By committing to ongoing education, refining your skills, and developing a long-term mindset, you'll be well-prepared for success in 2025 and beyond. Embrace the learning process, stay resilient in the face of setbacks, and remember that every experience—whether positive or negative—contributes to your growth as an options trader.

In an environment where change is constant, your dedication to responsible, informed, and disciplined trading will be your most valuable asset.

---

www.ingramcontent.com/pod-product-compliance
Lightning Source LLC
Chambersburg PA
CBHW071456220526
45472CB00003B/816